SOUL MATTERS

for Women

Wisdom & Inspiration
for the Most Important
Issues of Your Life

Copyright © 2005 by Mark Gilroy Communications, Tulsa, Oklahoma

Published by J. Countryman® a division of Thomas Nelson, Inc., Nashville, Tennessee 37214

Managing editor: Jessica Inman

For a list of acknowledgements, see pages 254-255.

Unless otherwise indicated, Scripture quotations are taken from *The Holy Bible*,
New Century Version, copyright © 1987, 1988, 1991 by Word Publishing,
Dallas, Texas 75039. Used by permission.

Scriptures marked NKJV are taken from The New King James Version.
Copyright © 1979, 1980, 1982, Thomas Nelson, Inc.

Scripture quotations marked CEV are taken from the Contemporary English Version,
copyright © 1991, 1992, 1995 by the American Bible Society. Used by permission.

www.jcountryman.com
www.thomasnelson.com

Designed by Jackson Design Company LLC, Springdale, Arkansas

ISBN #1404102027

Printed in China

SOUL
MATTERS
for Women

A Division of Thomas Nelson Publishers
Since 1798

www.thomasnelson.com

Contents

Take Care of Your Soul

What good is it if someone gains the whole world—but loses their soul?

In our mad-dash, non-stop way of life, we too often forget about—or blatantly ignore—what matters most for our lives. But deep down, the simple truth that nothing—no achievements, no pleasures, no possessions—equals the value of the human soul, resonates in our inner being. Because what we most want for ourselves is to live our lives with significance and meaning. We long to be all that God created us to be.

If you have found yourself too busy and too distracted by the hundreds of things that clamor for your attention to seek nourishment for your soul; if you have been simply going through the motions of fulfilling God's best plans for your life; if you are ready to stop floating with the currents of a joyless and shallow society in order to see a remarkable difference in your life—and profoundly impact the lives of those around you—then *Soul Matters for Women* is for you.

Soul Matters for Women tackles almost fifty of the crucial life issues women face, weaving together poignant personal reflection questions, inspirational quotes, real life stories from others, God's promises, brief—but hard-hitting—Bible studies, practical life application ideas, and prayer starters to help you to discover for yourself how to let your soul take flight and soar!

Where the soul is full of peace and joy, outward surrounding
and circumstances are of comparatively little account.

HANNAH WHITHALL SMITH

User's Guide

SOUL MATTERS FOR WOMEN *is easy to follow and use, but to maximize the benefit you get from this resource, here are a few quick ideas and suggestions for your consideration.*

TO THINK ABOUT

In any area of study, when we understand how a topic relates to our specific circumstances, we experience increased levels of interest, comprehension, and retention. When you ask yourself the questions with each topic, take your time and reflect on recent events in your own life.

LESSON FOR LIFE

These quick, hard-hitting, to-the-point Bible studies are not designed to provide you with everything you need to know and "all the answers" on each of the topics, but they are designed to stimulate your own thinking and discovery learning. You will enhance what is provided here when you take the extra time to look up all the Bible passages that are referenced.

"God Will" Promises

One of the ways our souls take flight is when we truly believe in our hearts that God is good and faithful. These life-changing promises have been embraced and experienced by women of faith for centuries and have stood the test of time. When one of the promises is particularly relevant to your life, take a few extra minutes to memorize the verse so it will always be close to your heart.

REAL LIFE

True life stories are an inspiring way to see how God is at work in the life of others. Some of these stories will be exactly what you need to make some important life changes and decisions. But you don't have to relate to every single person's story to discover dynamics that will help you experience God's presence more fully in your life.

ACTION

Not every Action Step found in *Soul Matters for Women* will be just right for you. But don't be afraid to stretch yourself and try something you would not normally think of on your own. Or let the ideas found with each soul matter prompt you to come up with an even better way to put truth into practice.

PRAYER

Let this brief prayer starter help you express your own requests, thanksgiving, and praise to God.

SERVANTHOOD

TRUE GREATNESS IS NOT DEFINED BY WHAT WE GET BUT BY WHAT WE GIVE.

*To serve is beautiful, but only
if it is done with joy and a
whole heart and a free mind.*

PEARL S. BUCK

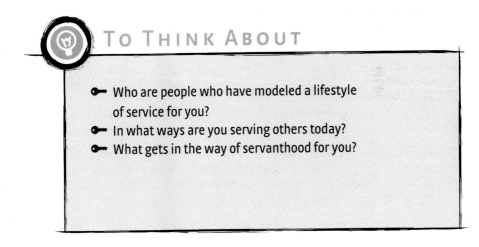

TO THINK ABOUT

- Who are people who have modeled a lifestyle of service for you?
- In what ways are you serving others today?
- What gets in the way of servanthood for you?

LESSON FOR LIFE

The Towel and Basin Society

BIBLE STUDY PASSAGE: JOHN 13:1-20

If I, your Lord and Teacher, have washed your feet, you also should wash each other's feet. I did this as an example so that you should do as I have done for you.

JOHN 13:14-15

One of the issues that most mattered to Jesus' disciples was who of them was the most favored and important to Him. In fact, two of the disciples, James and John, asked their mother to help them assume the seats of honor in Jesus' kingdom. Her request to Jesus was: "Promise that one of my sons will sit at your right side and the other will sit at your left side in your kingdom" (Matthew 20:21).

Jesus' response was that she didn't know what she was asking. She and her sons were interested in the trappings and benefits of power, but not the sacrifice. Otherwise, these sons of Zebedee could have been on Jesus' left and right when he prayed in the Garden (Matthew 26:40-46).

Instead, they slept. They could have been on His left and right when He was arrested (Mark 14:50). Instead, they fled.

They could have been on His left and right when He hung on a cross (Matthew 15:27, Luke 23:49, John 19:16-19, 26). Instead, they stayed in the crowd.

When Jesus taught His disciples the true meaning of greatness, He taught with a towel and basin. He washed their feet—the duty of a house servant. Peter, still unable to comprehend the object lesson, initially refused to let Jesus lower himself in such a way.

We live in a competitive and self-aggrandizing world. Examples of humility, kindness, helpfulness, and caring for others first—servanthood—are hard to find.

Great is the reward, the sense of purpose, the self satisfaction of one who follows the Master's example as a member of the "Towel and Basin Society."

Whoever makes himself great will be made humble. Whoever makes himself humble will be made great.

Matthew 23:12

 REAL LIFE

Confessions of a Martha

KATHRYN LAY

It was our third Thanksgiving dinner for the students in our English as a Second Language class, and we had a bigger crowd than ever. One hundred men, women, and children from over a dozen different countries had crowded into the fellowship area at the church.

Being an organized person, I'm almost always thrown into the Martha role: planning, preparing, setting up, and cleaning up for activities in the ministry. Being a shy person, I rarely take on a Mary role of mixing and mingling.

As the directors of the ministry, our family arrived early. I threw myself into setting up tables, covering them with richly colored cloths, and making sure there were plenty of dishes. By the time the other volunteers arrived, most of the setup work was done.

I was exhausted even before the meal began. As the students began arriving, there were lots of laughter and hugs. I watched in growing resentment as many of the other women in the ministry visited with the women students and their children.

I let my irritation take control, ruining my chances of ministering to anyone.

The meal was a success. We ate and talked and listened to my husband and others speak about our Thanksgiving traditions and being thankful to God for bringing us all together. But I felt anything but thankful as the party ended and the cleanup began. I carried food and empty plates to the trash and bowls to be washed to the sink, and moved tables and chairs back to where they came from. This time, there were other helpers. Yet I watched with sourness as many of the women sat and laughed with the students.

I knew they were being "Marys," ministering to the students, becoming their friends.

Why can't I be doing that instead of all this boring and hard work? I thought.

The bitterness I carried was painful, and I know it grieved the Lord, for it grieved me as I saw myself reacting in such an angry way.

As I helped stack the last of the folding chairs, one of our Kurdish students walked up to me.

"I thank you for being so hard a worker. I enjoy this Thanksgiving much," she said, kissing my cheeks graciously.

Other students made an effort to thank me before they left. I was reminded that God made me the way I am—a Martha.

I was amazed and grateful at how much God loves me that He would send a Kurdish student to remind me where I am most comfortable and where my talents and strengths are used best.

Being a Martha is a blessing. People may not notice the details of a well-run event, but disorganization and chaos can hurt the special moments of such a ministry.

And I've found that I can still listen to another and speak words of friend-ship while my hands are in dishwater.

ACTION STEP

MANY PEOPLE ARE HELPED IN THEIR SPIRITUAL LIFE BY KEEPING RELIGIOUS SYMBOLS IN VIEW. A BIBLE ON THE COFFEE TABLE, FOR EXAMPLE, CAN INDICATE THE IMPORTANCE OF GOD'S WORD TO A FAMILY. A SINGLE CROSS CAN BE A POWERFUL REMINDER OF REDEMPTION THROUGH JESUS' BLOOD. WHAT WOULD BE A SYMBOL OF SERVANTHOOD THAT WOULD REMIND AND ENCOURAGE YOU TO REACH OUT IN SERVICE TO OTHERS? A TOWEL AND BASIN? CREATE YOUR OWN PERSONAL REMINDER OF THE JOY OF SERVANT-HOOD.

PRAYER

Thank You, God, for sending Jesus into my life and heart with the gift of salvation. Help me to honor that gift through service to others.

YOUR FUTURE

WHEN WE ARE GOING THROUGH TOUGH TIMES WE MUST REMEMBER THAT OUR FUTURE IS IN GOD'S HANDS.

Life is God's novel. Let Him write it.

ISAAC BASHEVIS SINGER

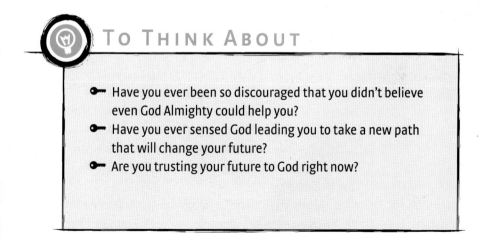

TO THINK ABOUT

- Have you ever been so discouraged that you didn't believe even God Almighty could help you?
- Have you ever sensed God leading you to take a new path that will change your future?
- Are you trusting your future to God right now?

LESSON FOR LIFE

Promises

God Will:

Reveal Himself
Proverbs 2:3-5

Bring success
Proverbs 16:3

Hear your prayers
1 John 5:14

Carry out His plan
for your life
Jeremiah 29:11

A Future and a Hope

BIBLE STUDY PASSAGE: JOHN 10:10-16

"I know what I am planning for you," says the Lord.
"I have good plans for you, not plans to hurt you.
I will give you hope and a good future."

JEREMIAH 29:11

Jeremiah is known as the "weeping prophet." Imagine losing absolutely everything you hold dear—your family, home, country, church, and maybe even your faith. Jeremiah anguished over what had happened to his people. King Nebuchadnezzar had conquered the Kingdom of Judah, destroying the walls of Jerusalem and the temple built by Solomon. The strongest and most educated were led as captives to serve the conquering king. They left behind all they loved, smoldering in ruins.

This young man of God preached to the Hebrew exiles, who now lived in the foreign country of Babylon, along the banks of the Tigris River.

Like Job who had lost future and family; like Joseph and their Hebrew ancestors who were captives in Egypt, despair

18

reigned in the lives of the Israelites—their hope was lost. How could they think of themselves as God's chosen people under such circumstances?

In the midst of this hopelessness, this young prophet, Jeremiah, called to speak for God at an early age, dried his eyes and boldly proclaimed a new promise—that God had a future filled with hope for these people. That promise did come true for the Hebrew children, and the promise still echoes and holds true today, no matter what the situation in which you find yourself.

Do things look bleak in your life right now? Are you flooded with insecurity about the future? Just as God had a plan for His people thousands of years ago, He has a plan for you—a good, pleasing, and perfect plan. And He is trustworthy to make that plan happen.

Lord, I know that a person's life doesn't really belong to him. No one can control his own life.
Jeremiah 10:23

REAL LIFE

God Knew

STEFFANIE CLIFTON

In Psalm 40:2, David says, "He lifted me out of the pit of destruction, out of the sticky mud. He stood me on a rock and made my feet steady." I cannot reflect on my life without seeing the ways God has made my feet steady in my family and career.

While contemplating my future at the behest of guidance counselors and teachers in high school, I could never have imagined the life I have now. I would have laughed then if you'd told me I was cut out to be a well-paid and recognized business leader, quickly climbing the corporate ladder. I would have laughed at the notion of my current life when I was living in a roach-infested house, fearing harassing creditors with every phone call, only days away from declaring bankruptcy.

I remember shopping with food stamps, while living in the "roach motel" with little to no furniture. I remember driving a car with nothing under my feet—the floorboard had fallen out due to rust and wear. I remember working as a waitress at a pizza joint after declaring bankruptcy. With the natural eye, things looked bleak, but God knew what He was doing.

He also knew what He was doing when He introduced me to a caring, loving man who listened to God and supported me as I followed God's plan for my life. Over the eleven years of our marriage, my husband, Ken, has encouraged me as I took steps that have led me toward success. He was there for me as I applied for a pizza delivery job that turned into an assistant manager job that turned into a general manager job. He was there for me, later, when I applied for an assistant manager job at one of my favorite retail stores, which turned into a general manager job, and led to a promotion to a position at the company's corporate headquarters. In each step, he had the optimism to believe more strongly in my future than I did. I can really see the heart of Jesus in Ken's support of me, and it warms my heart to know God supports me even more than he does.

Finally, God knew what he was doing when He led Ken and me to examine our lives six years ago and realize that our personal talents and interests meant we should "switch places" as wage earner and caretaker. I never could have planned all this, but God knew all along what would make me happy and was at work to get me there.

In my life, there are still hectic and crazed periods, especially at the end of a long work week; however, I can find peace and joy in knowing that, even now, God knows what He's doing and is leading me in a plan for success and happiness.

ACTION STEP

IN A JOURNAL OR A BLANK SHEET OF PAPER, WRITE A LIST OF NINE THINGS YOU WOULD LOVE TO BE PART OF YOUR FUTURE. NUMBER EACH OF THEM AND THEN WRITE DOWN THE NUMBER "10." NEXT TO THAT, WRITE, "WHATEVER GOD WANTS FOR ME." COMMIT THE LIST TO GOD AND PUT IT IN A SAFE PLACE FOR FUTURE REFERENCE.

PRAYER

I do not know what is next in my life, but God, I trust in Your love and Your promises, and believe in my heart that a bright future awaits me.

A SPIRIT OF GENEROSITY

GOD CALLS US TO SHARE FROM OUR ABUNDANCE WITH THOSE IN NEED—EVEN WHEN WE FEEL NEEDY OURSELVES.

*Seeing our Father in everything makes life
one long thanksgiving and gives rest of the heart.*

HANNAH WHITHALL SMITH

TO THINK ABOUT

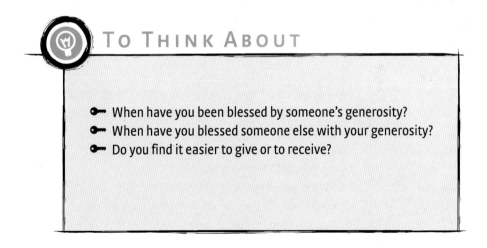

- When have you been blessed by someone's generosity?
- When have you blessed someone else with your generosity?
- Do you find it easier to give or to receive?

LESSON FOR LIFE

Promises

God will:

Enrich your life in all
ways
Deuteronomy 30:19-20
John 10:10

Make you joyful through
giving
2 Corinthians 9:7

Bless your obedience
Psalm 119:2

Multiply your gifts
Luke 6:38

Never leave you
Hebrews 13:5

The Gift of Giving

BIBLE STUDY PASSAGE: ROMANS 12:1-10

"Bring to the storehouse a full tenth of what you earn so there will be food in my house. Test me in this," says the Lord All-Powerful. "I will open the windows of heaven for you and pour out all the blessings you need."

MALACHI 3:10

One of the true tests of our character is what we do with our money. Of course, God calls us to give a portion of our income to Him through ministry (Numbers 18:28) and to also give special sacrificial offerings to meet special needs as we feel directed in our hearts (Numbers 15:3). Paul does say that some people have a special gift of giving (Romans 12:8), but he also points out that God loves a cheerful giver (2 Corinthians 9:7), and Jesus himself drew attention to the meager—but beautiful—gift of a poor widow as a true model of generosity all of us should follow (Matthew 12:43-44).

When we are generous with our money above and beyond expectations, a number of healthy emotional and spiritual dynamics are fostered in our lives—

- *We acknowledge that God owns everything and we have only been appointed as caretakers. The psalmist declares on behalf of God: "Every animal of the forest is already mine. The cattle on a thousand hills are mine" (Psalm 50:10).*
- *We clutch less tightly to what we can generate and become more aware that all good gifts come from God. James tells us: "Every perfect gift is from God." (James 1:17).*
- *We learn to trust and serve God with a pure heart. Jesus told his disciples: "You cannot serve both God and worldly riches" (Matthew 6:24).*
- *We receive the joy that comes from helping someone in need (Matthew 25:23).*
- *We become more confident and trusting, and begin to eliminate worry from our lives (Philippians 4:5-7, 17).*
- *We become better stewards in all areas of our finances; there is a strange paradox that the more we give the more we seem to have (Matthew 19:29).*

Whoever gives to others will get richer; those who help others will themselves be helped.
Proverbs 11:25

The most important gift that God wants you to offer Him is your very life (Romans 12:1-2). Then He can teach you the wonderful truth that whatever we grasp and hoard, dries up and suffocates. Whatever we give freely and generously, takes off and soars.

REAL LIFE

Treasures in Heaven

NANETTE THORSEN-SNIPES

I found out the day before my twenty-second wedding anniversary that my husband, Jim, had lost his job.

Easing into a kitchen chair, I listened while Jim explained. Like so many other people we knew, his job had been downsized. After twenty-six years in a middle management position from which he'd planned to retire, he was let go without warning.

Five years later, a week following my birthday, he was laid off again. Trauma set in as Jim digested the news. Both layoffs were a time of testing, and we learned hard lessons in the process. We gave up many temporal treasures of our hearts—newer vehicles, another home, vacations, furniture, and more. Unlike the first job loss, though, our second unemployment found us floating in a sea of medical bills, making despair a more formidable threat than ever before.

Jim and I worked hard keeping depression at bay. Jim began every day with Bible reading and prayer. He made a list of who he was in Christ, things like: *Jesus can manage my future because He is in charge; I stand firm in Jesus; and the Lord is my confidence, what shall I fear?* At one point, we read through the Psalms together.

During Jim's first layoff, Hurricane Mitch had ripped into Honduras leaving people with no homes, food, or clothing. While I sat watching TV coverage of the disaster, God burdened my heart for all those people. Although we didn't have much, I convinced Jim to focus on the Lord's will rather than our situation. We gathered clothes and canned goods and took them to a nearby church. While we stood in the church basement talking to the pastor, I felt God prompt me to write a check for $100—money we could ill afford to give.

Later during our time of need, an e-mail friend from Texas sent a card with a crisp $100 bill inside. She wrote a note saying that her father had sold some cattle, and she wanted us to have some of the proceeds. I believed her since she was from Texas—until I reread the card. It was our Father who provided the blessing, our Father who owns the cattle on a thousand hills. This was an opportunity to learn how to receive—something we learned could sometimes be harder than giving.

Stepping out in faith and obedience to God's call by giving sacrificially was our starting point. For a couple of hours one day, we stepped outside ourselves and our bleak situation and gave to someone else. Not only did it feel good to give to "the least of these," we knew it was God's will.

We continued to tithe on everything that God provided. We praised God for everything, even for the job losses, and we continued to give to those less fortunate. And God was faithful to meet our needs in special, unexpected ways. We have truly stored up for ourselves treasures in heaven.

ACTION STEP

LOOK FOR A SPECIAL NEED IN YOUR COMMUNITY, NEIGHBORHOOD, OR
CHURCH. ASK GOD TO IMPRESS ON YOUR HEART WHAT YOU CAN GIVE TO
BLESS THAT PERSON OR FAMILY IN THEIR SITUATION. IF AT ALL POSSIBLE, MAKE
YOUR GIFT IN SECRET AND KEEP IT BETWEEN YOU AND GOD.

PRAYER

*I praise You, O God, who meets all my needs and lavishes me with all kinds of
blessings. Thank You for enabling me to be generous with others.*

SHARING MY FAITH

WE ARE CALLED TO TELL OTHERS WHAT GREAT THINGS GOD HAS DONE IN OUR HEARTS AND LIVES.

*Insomuch as anyone pushes you nearer
to God, he or she is your friend.*

ANONYMOUS

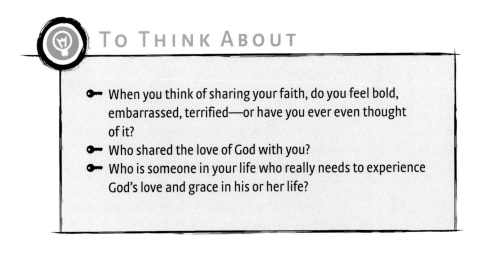

To Think About

- When you think of sharing your faith, do you feel bold, embarrassed, terrified—or have you ever even thought of it?
- Who shared the love of God with you?
- Who is someone in your life who really needs to experience God's love and grace in his or her life?

LESSON FOR LIFE

Promises

God will:

Make you a fisher of men
Mark 1:17

Save those who call
on him
Romans 10:19

Use you to point others
to God
Daniel 12:3

Prepare in advance for
your good works
Ephesians 2:10

A Story to Tell

BIBLE STUDY PASSAGE: ACTS 8:26-40

Love your neighbor as you love yourself.

MARK 12:31

The last recorded words of Jesus before His ascension into heaven were: "But when the Holy Spirit comes to you, you will receive power. You will be my witnesses—in Jerusalem, in all of Judea, in Samaria, and in every part of the world" (Acts 1:8).

One of the lessons Jesus wanted His disciples to hear was that they need to share their story of God's love to those closest to them (Jerusalem), those in their general vicinity (Samaria), and ultimately to the ends of the earth.

There are a number of hindrances to sharing our faith—

- *Some people have been "burned" by someone who attends church and are highly resistant to the gospel.*
- *Some of us feel embarrassed to talk about God, fearing others might think we are strange—or be offended by our words.*
- *Some of us are not confident in our knowledge of the Bible and spiritual matters.*

There are a few dynamics of sharing your faith that might help you relax and be more effective—

- *First, it is not our job to convince people that they are sinners who are going to hell without God. It is the job of the Holy Spirit to convict people of their need for God (Matthew 10:19-20).*
- *Second, God will guide us to people who are open and receptive and ready to hear about God's love. Paul was led to a city in Macedonia by a divine dream (Acts 16:9). An angel led Philip to an Ethiopian politician (Acts 8:26-27). He will lead you to people who are responsive to your story.*
- *Third, not all of us are called to be evangelists, but all of us are called to be witnesses (Acts 1:8). What does a witness do? Simple. She tells her story. You don't have to teach a Bible lesson or understand theology to tell your story. You just have to know what God has done for you.*
- *Fourth, the Holy Spirit gives us special power when we share the love of God with others. If you stumble and bumble a little bit, don't worry. The Holy Spirit is at work, too.*

Are you ready to share? Keep it simple. In the words of Peter, "Always be ready to answer everyone who asks you to explain about the hope you have" (1 Peter 3:15).

Because the Good News we brought to you came not only with words, but with power, with the Holy Spirit, and with sure knowledge that it is true. Also you know how we lived when we were with you in order to help you.
1 Thessalonians 1:5

31

 REAL LIFE

Love Your Neighbor

KAREN R. KILBY

Our new next-door neighbor was a single working mom in her thirties, with teenage children close in age to ours. Gail was an attractive, well-dressed woman with a hat to match every outfit—her trademark which set her apart in the highly competitive real estate market in which she worked. Getting to know Gail was easy. We would often meet at the mailboxes at the end of our driveways or while working out in our yards. From what Gail heard from the other neighbors, she thought we were a religious family and brought God into our conversations on several occasions.

One morning while visiting in our home, Gail commented, "I feel something different in your home. You know, as a realtor, I am in many homes and I don't sense in them what I feel here. I can feel love in every room in this house."

I was touched by her compliment of God's love being so evident.

As we continued to get better acquainted over the next few weeks, I sensed Gail did not have an intimate relationship with God. I began to pray and ask, *God, how can I introduce Gail to You?* His answer came with another question. *Why don't you roll up that talk you gave at the Christian Women's Club luncheon, tie it with a red ribbon, and put it in her mailbox?* That sounded like a great idea to me, so I did.

The following day I found a smaller scroll tied with a red ribbon placed in my mailbox. As I slipped off the ribbon, I read Gail's message. "I was touched by what you have shared and have decided to accept God into my life—what's next?" Soon our mailboxes bulged with books being constantly passed back and forth as Gail eagerly absorbed as much as she could. As fast as Gail finished reading one book, I would give her another, prompting meaningful discussions of a daily walk with God. Our friendship deepened as we became tied together with His love.

A few years later, Gail moved away. Not long after, I heard of her untimely death and was saddened to know I had lost this special friend. As I mourned her loss, a refrain from a hymn—"blessed be the tie that binds our hearts in Christian love"—reminded me that God was still the tie that would bind our hearts for all time. How glad I was that I had responded to God's perfect timing to love my neighbor with a scroll tied with His red ribbon of love.

ACTION STEP

TO BETTER PREPARE YOURSELF TO BE A WITNESS OF GOD'S LOVE, WORK ON
TWO DYNAMICS OF SHARING—

1. WRITE OUT YOUR BEFORE-AND-AFTER STORY. DESCRIBE YOUR LIFE
BEFORE CHRIST; TELL HOW YOU CAME TO REALIZE YOUR NEED FOR
CHRIST; AND THEN SHARE HOW YOUR LIFE IS DIFFERENT SINCE
ACCEPTING CHRIST INTO YOUR HEART.
2. VISIT A CHRISTIAN BOOKSTORE OR GO TO CHRISTIAN WEBSITES ONLINE
AND LOOK AT SOME OF THE SIMPLE GUIDES TO LEADING SOMEONE TO
CHRIST: THE FOUR SPIRITUAL LAWS, THE ROMAN ROAD, ETC. SELECT ONE
AND FAMILIARIZE YOURSELF WITH WHAT YOU WOULD SAY TO SOMEONE
WHO WANTS TO KNOW JESUS CHRIST.

PRAYER

*I'm forever grateful, O Lord, for the gift of salvation You give to me. Lead me to
someone who needs to experience your love and grace.*

QUIET TIMES

IN THE HUSTLE AND BUSTLE OF LIFE, WE NEED STILL, QUIET MOMENTS TO BE ALONE WITH GOD.

*You are not obliged to put on
evening clothes to meet God.*

AUSTIN O'MALLEY

TO THINK ABOUT

- How often do you experience "quietness" in your life? How much is on purpose?
- What are the biggest distractions in your life?
- How would your life change if you spent even a little time each day in silent reflection?

LESSON FOR LIFE

Promises

God will:

Renew your heart
Ezekiel 36:26-27

Restore your soul
Psalm 23:3

Preserve and renew your
spirit
2 Corinthians 4:16

Draw close to you
James 4:8

Away from the Crowds

BIBLE STUDY PASSAGE: JOHN 4:1-11

*Pray in the Spirit at all times with all kinds of prayers,
asking for everything you need. To do this you must
always be ready and never give up. Always pray for all
God's people.*

EPHESIANS 6:18

If you read through the four Gospels you can't help but
notice how people—and crowds—were drawn to Jesus. If He
went up a hill to pray alone, the crowds would be gathered
below awaiting His return (Luke 4:42). If He jumped into a boat
to slip off to the other side of a lake, word of His movements
would race Him to the other side (Matthew 14:13). He interacted non-stop with military officers, widows, children, the
seriously ill, the demon-possessed, religious leaders, close
friends, prophets, and sinners.

At the beginning of His ministry at age thirty, despite
having so much to do in such a short amount of time for His
Father in heaven, Jesus pulled away from everyone to spend
forty days in the wilderness to pray and fast. While alone, Jesus

was tested three times by Satan, but each time answered the challenge with Scripture and a profound sense of His purpose in life (Matthew 4:1-11).

Again, at the end of his earthly life, Jesus pulled away from the crowds to pray alone in the Garden of Gethsemane (Mark 14:35-36). It was there, with the agony of the cross just before Him, that He reaffirmed His most earnest desire: "Not My will, but Yours, be done" (Luke 22:42 NKJV).

If Jesus Christ sought solitude and quiet, how much more important is it for us? We can come to the end of the day—or week or even month—and discover that we made no time at all to be alone with God. Television, radio, meetings, chores, and a cacophony of other "noises" crowd out prayer and silent reflection.

You don't have to take a forty-day trip to the desert to create ways to spend quiet time alone with God. In fact, once you recognize what distracts you from hearing God's voice, it's just a matter of giving yourself some quiet time. Your soul will thrive as you pull away from the noise to hear the voice of your Father.

Create in me a pure heart, God, and make my spirit right again.
Psalm 51:10

 REAL LIFE

A Sunshine Day

GLENDA PALMER

I glanced at the paper magnetized to the refrigerator: *High School Beach Party Saturday 10 – 3.*

It's almost three now, I thought. *I better run.*

As I drove to the church, random thoughts about the rest of the day filled my mind: I've got to go to the grocery store before dinner. I wonder if Jeannie remembered her flute lesson.

I pulled in a parking space in front of the church. *Just as I thought: They aren't back yet, and I didn't even bring anything to read.*

Ten minutes later, I was becoming more uncomfortable. It's so hot in the car. If the church auditorium is open, I could get a drink of cold water.

I looked down at my old denim shorts and faded top. *I hope no one sees me like this.*

I got out, walked up the cement stairs, and tried the huge front door. That's lucky, I thought as the door opened easily. Strolling across the foyer to the drinking fountain, I glanced into the dark auditorium.

This water is sure good and it's a lot cooler in here. I wonder if anyone else is around.

"Hello?" No one answered, so I walked into the auditorium. I had never been in the church when it was dark and empty. It had always been filled with nicely-dressed worshipers, angelic choir members, and kind ushers. It was so silent and dim now—except for a bright spot of light shining right on the center pews.

I wonder what that light is. It looks like it is coming from the balcony. I walked slowly down the aisle looking back to see if I could find the source.

"Wow, look at that! Oh, how beautiful—how beautiful," I breathed.

The small balcony was aglow with a rainbow of colors. The ceiling, floor, pews, songbooks, and even my faded white shirt were covered with bright reds, blues, yellows, and greens as the sunlight shone through each piece of leaded glass. As I tiptoed over to the window and touched its warmth, I gazed at the blood-red reflection on my hand. Swallowing, I looked at the simple cross in the center with rows of varied-colored glass jewels framing it. Each tiny piece of hand-blown glass had been carefully cut and set in its own place to make a glorious, complete picture.

Alone in the silence, I knelt and prayed, "Oh, Lord, thank you for meeting with me here today. Forgive me for being too busy with worldly things to see your sacrifice and majesty every day. Remind me so I never forget. Amen."

Outside I could hear the squeaking brakes and loud, laughing teenagers. I took a deep breath and a last look at my stained glass window. Reluctantly I walked down the stairs.

A sandy, smiling boy was standing by the car with his surfboard and towel.

"It was great, Mom, and the waves were awesome!"

"I had an awesome day, too."

ACTION STEP

FASTING IS THE SPIRITUAL DISCIPLINE OF NOT PARTAKING OF FOOD FOR A SET PERIOD OF TIME IN ORDER TO DEVOTE OUR HEARTS AND MINDS TO SPIRITUAL MATTERS. BUT ABSTAINING FROM FOOD IS NOT THE ONLY PHYSICAL EXPRESSION OF FASTING. CONSIDER A ONE-, TWO-, OR THREE-DAY PERIOD OF NO RADIO, TV, OR OTHER "NOISE" IN YOUR HOME. (DISCUSS THIS WITH YOUR FAMILY FIRST!) REMEMBER, THE PURPOSE IS TO FOCUS OUR WHOLE HEART, SOUL, AND MIND ON GOD!

PRAYER

You speak to me through Your Word, and through pastors, and through books, but thank You, God, that You also speak to me in a quiet voice when I am silent before You.

GOD'S GRACE

GOD GIVES GOOD GIFTS TO HIS CHILDREN.

*Just as there comes a warm sunbeam into every cottage window,
so comes a love born of God's care for every separate need.*

NATHANIEL HAWTHORNE

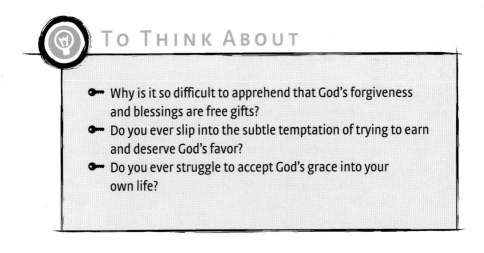

TO THINK ABOUT

- Why is it so difficult to apprehend that God's forgiveness and blessings are free gifts?
- Do you ever slip into the subtle temptation of trying to earn and deserve God's favor?
- Do you ever struggle to accept God's grace into your own life?

LESSON FOR LIFE

Riches of Grace

BIBLE STUDY PASSAGE: EPHESIANS 2:1-10

But he said to me, "My grace is enough for you. When you are weak, my power is made perfect in you." So I am very happy to brag about my weaknesses. Then Christ's power can live in me.

2 CORINTHIANS 12:9

Did you know God favors you? Not because you are the most beautiful; not because you are the smartest; not because you have lots of talents; not because you do many good deeds—though all of these characteristics may be abundant in your life!

No, God favors you out of His deep, abiding love for you, a love that is not contingent upon any effort you put forth. In fact, if you declared yourself to be God's enemy today, He would love you just as much.

God's grace is a wonderful reality that is available for you right now. Here are some aspects of grace that just might be what you need to hear today—

42

• *Grace means God loved you and knew you before you were even born. God said to Jeremiah: "Before I made you in your mother's womb, I chose you. Before you were born, I set you apart for a special work. I appointed you as a prophet to the nations" (Jeremiah 1:5).*

• *Grace provides the gift of salvation, a gift that can't be earned. Paul says: "You have been saved by grace through believing. You did not save yourselves; it was a gift from God" (Ephesians 2:8).*

• *Grace is available to us when we are weak. Paul says: "So I am very happy to brag about my weaknesses. Then Christ's power can live in me" (2 Corinthians 12:9).*

• *Grace is sufficient for absolutely any need we have—whether health, finances, relationships, temptations, or any other need. Paul says: "My grace is sufficient for you" (2 Corinthians 12:9 NKJV).*

• *Grace provides us with the strength we need to over come temptation and live a victorious Christian life. Says Peter, "Jesus has the power of God, by which he has given us everything we need to live and to serve God." (2 Peter 1:3).*

May the Lord show you his kindness and have mercy on you.
Numbers 6:25

Whatever need you have in your life today, be assured, God is on your side. He is ready and able to help you as you respond to Him with faith.

REAL LIFE

Joy on a Hot June Day

EDNA ELLISON

I spent the day before my daughter's wedding at the caterer, the florist, and the church—about forty miles away. I felt little joy as I watched my budget dwindle. My son, Jack, came home from college to walk his younger sister down the aisle, taking the place of his dad, who'd died a few years before. He teased Patsy, saying he'd wanted to give her away since she was three years old.

To save money, I gathered blossoms from a friend's magnolia trees for the flower arrangements. After the rehearsal dinner we banked the podium area with luscious magnolias. The next day, while Patsy dressed, her fiancé, Tim, walked with me to check the flowers. We felt a rush of hot air as we opened the sanctuary door. And then I saw them: All the beautiful white flowers were black. Funeral black. An overnight storm had knocked out the air conditioner, and on that hot June day of 107 degrees, the flowers had died.

I panicked, knowing I didn't have time to go home, gather more flowers, and return in time for the wedding.

Tim asked, "Can you get more flowers? I'll toss these dead ones and put in fresh flowers."

I mumbled, "Sure," as he bebopped down the hall to put on his cuff links.

Alone in the sanctuary, I prayed. *Lord, help me find flowers—in a hurry!* I asked for white magnolias, safety from biting dogs, and a friendly person who wouldn't get a shotgun when I asked to rip his tree to shreds!

Leaving the church, I saw magnolia trees in the distance. I approached a house with a giant magnolia tree and no dog in sight. I knocked on the door and an older man answered. He seemed happy to share his magnolias, handing me large boughs. Lifting the last armload into my car trunk, I said, "Sir, you've made the mother of a bride very happy."

"No," he said. "You don't understand what's happening."

"What?" I asked.

"You see, my wife of sixty-seven years died on Monday. On Wednesday—" I saw his tears welling up, "—I buried her." He looked away. "Yesterday my children left for Greenwood, where they live." I nodded in sympathy.

"This morning," he continued, "I was sitting in my den crying out loud. I miss her so much. She needed me, but now nobody needs me. This morning I cried aloud, 'Who needs an eighty-six-year-old, wore-out man? Nobody!' Then you knocked, and said, 'Sir, I need you!'

"As I gave you those flowers, I decided I'm needed. Why, I might have a flower ministry! You know what I'm going to do? Serve the Lord until He calls me home!"

I drove back to the church, overwhelmed by how God had met so many needs that day. Sometimes God's grace looks so simple and ordinary—like an eighty-six-year-old man with tear-filled eyes and a wide grin.

ACTION STEP

IN THE OLD TESTAMENT, THE ISRAELITES WERE TO CELEBRATE GOD'S DELIVER-
ANCE FROM EGYPT THROUGH A FEAST CALLED PASSOVER (NUMBERS 9:3). IN
THE NEW TESTAMENT, THE CHURCH WAS TO CELEBRATE THEIR DELIVERANCE
FROM SIN THROUGH PARTAKING OF THE LORD'S SUPPER (LUKE 22:19). WHAT
ADDITIONAL REMINDER OF GRACE CAN YOU POST IN YOUR HOME TO KEEP YOU
AWARE OF GOD'S FAVOR IN YOUR LIFE RIGHT NOW?

PRAYER

*I can never thank You enough or ever hope to repay even a small portion of the
ultimate gift You have given me through Jesus Christ's death and resurrection. I
cling to Your grace today.*

TRUE JOY

JOY IS A GIFT FROM GOD THAT GOES DEEPER THAN MERE HAPPINESS AND BEYOND ANY CIRCUMSTANCES.

Joy is the echo of God's life within us.

JOSEPH MARMION

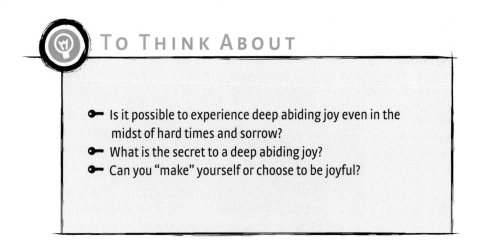

To Think About

- Is it possible to experience deep abiding joy even in the midst of hard times and sorrow?
- What is the secret to a deep abiding joy?
- Can you "make" yourself or choose to be joyful?

LESSON FOR LIFE

Promises

Joy Is Everywhere

BIBLE STUDY PASSAGE: GALATIANS 5:22-25

God will:

Good people, rejoice and be happy in the Lord. Sing all you

Give good gifts

whose hearts are right.

Psalm 84:11

PSALM 32:11

Ephesians 1:3

There are so many ways to experience God's joy in your

Bless those who trust

life. How many ways are you celebrating right now?

Him

Jeremiah 17:7

• *The joy of God's presence. In Psalm 16:8-9, David exalts: "I*

keep the Lord before me always. Because he is close by my side,

Make your heart joyful

I will not be hurt. So I rejoice and am glad." If God is beside you,

Psalm 4:7

no one can steal that joy.

• *The joy of salvation. Paul tells us: "And not only that, but now*

Bring joy even in the

we are also very happy in God through our Lord Jesus Christ.

midst of difficulties

Through him we are now God's friends again" (Romans 5:11).

James 1:2-3

Forgiveness of sins and peace with God are great reasons to be

joyful.

• *The joy of God's goodness. Isaiah 63:9 tells us of God's great*

redemptive work: "When they suffered, he suffered also. He sent

his own angel to save them. Because of his love and kindness, he saved them. Since long ago he has picked them up and carried them." What a kind and good God—and what a great source of joy!

• *The joy of God's Word.* King David speaks of God's Word with awe, reverence, and joy: "I delight to do Your will, O my God, and Your law is within my heart" (Psalm 40:8 NKJV). Do you set yourself up for joy each day by partaking of God's Word?

• *The joy of a clean heart.* One of the most beautiful prayers ever uttered was David's immortal prayer for cleansing: "Create in me a pure heart, God, and make my spirit right again. Do not send me away from you or take your Holy Spirit away from me. Give me back the joy of your salvation. Keep me strong by giving me a willing spirit" (Psalm 51:10-12). If you are not experiencing joy in your life, maybe you need to start by seeking God's forgiveness and cleansing.

• *Joy in suffering.* It doesn't seem possible to experience joy in the midst of sorrow, but Jesus reminded His disciples, "In the world you will have tribulation; but be of good cheer, I have overcome the world" (John 16:33 NKJV).

Are you discouraged? Blue? Depressed? Don't forget—joy is everywhere!

Crying may last for a night, but joy comes in the morning.
Psalm 30:5

 REAL LIFE

What Does Joy Look Like?

CAROL HARRISON

Commotion woke the three-year-old early that crisp October morning. Her pudgy toes reached for the floor as she slipped from her bed to investigate. Daddy was talking to the telephone. "She won't wake up. She's limp and unresponsive," he insisted. Mommy was sitting in the big chair holding a roll of blankets that contained the long-awaited baby sister. The toddler appraised the scene with big, wide-awake eyes. Fear crept into her little heart as she realized something was very wrong.

She stood in the doorway remembering her excitement the day before when Mommy and Daddy brought the baby home. Daddy had lifted her into the big chair and Mommy placed the animated doll into her arms. "Her name is Joy," Mommy had said. "She's your baby sister." The older sibling's tummy filled with butterflies of delight. She giggled as the newborn infant wriggled its mouth and tiny fingers. She had never held a doll like this one.

What had changed? What was happening this morning?

Daddy brushed by her to answer the knock at the door. It was the pastor and his wife, Doris. They had never come for breakfast. This was an unusual day. Doris scooped up the frightened little girl for the tightest hug ever. After they all gathered around Mommy in the big chair, the pastor began to pray for the baby. "God, you brought Joy into the world. You brought Joy into this family. Reach down and touch this child with your mercy and healing." While big sister did not understand the prayer, she said a hearty "Amen" at the end. But she was not prepared for what happened next.

Mommy, Daddy, and the pastor took her precious Joy back to the hospital. Standing at the screen door, she sobbed into the cold air, "I just knew we couldn't keep her!" Painful sadness blanketed her. Mommy and Daddy could not promise they would bring her Joy back to her. They did not know. The sensitive pastor's wife led the child back to the big chair. They waited for the return of Mommy and Daddy. She explained the power of prayer. After they asked God to protect and heal little Joy, the sadness began to lift and the tears began to dry. The butterflies fluttered once again in her tummy. She returned to the screen door, but this time she was waiting for her little sister to return. Somehow she knew her Joy would be back.

And Joy came back. Joy came when God's hand reached down to stop a cerebral hemorrhage in an infant baby. Joy came as God's peace and comfort when life became too difficult to bear. Joy came through the smile on a toddler's face when the animated doll was placed back into her arms. Joy came through the beautiful, purpose-filled woman who makes our family complete. Joy looks like my sister.

ACTION STEP

CAN YOU DECIDE TO BE JOYFUL? ACCORDING TO MANY OF THE SCRIPTURES ABOVE, JOY IS AT LEAST IN PART A DECISION. DECIDE TODAY TO—

- THANK GOD FOR SALVATION.
- PRAISE GOD FOR HIS PRESENCE.
- CELEBRATE GOD'S GOODNESS.
- WORSHIP GOD WITH A SENSE OF JOY.
- ENJOY GOD'S WORD.
- SEEK GOD'S JOY THROUGH CLEANSING.
- TRUST GOD FOR JOY IN TRIBULATION.

PRAYER

I delight in You, O Lord. You are my source of true joy. Thank You for making my heart glad!

FRIENDSHIP

ONE OF THE GREATEST SOURCES OF COMFORT AND JOY IS GOD'S GIFT OF FRIENDSHIP.

God makes our lives a medley of joy and tears,
hope and help, love and encouragement.

AUTHOR UNKNOWN

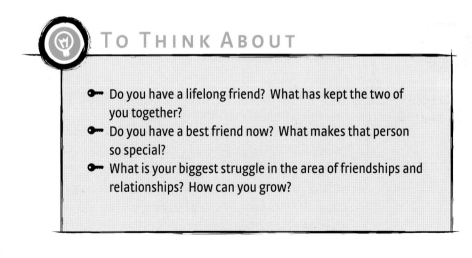

TO THINK ABOUT

- Do you have a lifelong friend? What has kept the two of you together?
- Do you have a best friend now? What makes that person so special?
- What is your biggest struggle in the area of friendships and relationships? How can you grow?

LESSON FOR LIFE

Promises

God will:

Be your Friend

John 15:15

Never leave you

Hebrews 13:5

Be with you as you meet

with other believers

Matthew 18:20

We Need Each Other!

BIBLE STUDY PASSAGE: 1 SAMUEL 18:1-4

Pleasant words are like a honeycomb, making people happy and healthy.

PROVERBS 16:24

Did you know that friendship fights stress? Shelley Taylor, Ph.D., professor of psychology at UCLA, says about women, "We're more inclined to seek out friends and reach out to family. Social support brings down our blood pressure, signals our adrenal glands to stop pumping out corticosteroids, and voila! We feel less anxious, less overwrought, less over-whelmed. We may even live longer as a result of coping this way: Taylor says the friendship response to stress may explain why women outlive men" (Ladies Home Journal).

Do you have enough friends in your life to stay healthy? Emotionally? Mentally? Spiritually?

One of the most dramatic stories of friendship in the Bible is that of David and Jonathan. David, once King Saul's favorite, has become the target of the king's growing madness and wrath. Jonathan, torn between love for his father and his friend, ultimately obeys God and at great personal risk and cost, protects David on numerous occasions. David reciprocates that love by sparing Saul's life on two occasions—and blessing Jonathan's children and grandchildren.

Sometimes friendship expresses more intense love than that we share with our family. But without exception, all of us need the support of someone we trust and whom we can share our joys, sorrows, challenges, and heart with.

A true friend is someone to cry with as a comfort in times of trouble; someone to laugh with in order to rekindle joy; someone to pray with to lift our spirits.; someone to argue with as we challenge each other to grow and be our best; someone to share hearts with us so that we can know them and ourselves better; someone to forgive and be forgiven by as we learn about God's redemptive love for us; someone to grow old with as we become women of wisdom and grace together.

In other words, friends are good for the soul.

A man who has friends must himself be friendly, but there is a friend who sticks closer than a brother.
Proverbs 18:24 NKJV

55

 REAL LIFE

Lord, Send Me a Friend

ANNETTEE BUDZBAN

I had just been through great amounts of loss in my life. I'd lost an old friend, my father, my oldest sister, my health, and my nursing career. I couldn't believe it when I received another heartbreaking phone call.

"I have some news for you. My husband was just offered a new job in another state, and he accepted," the voice on the other end said.

This call was from my friend Sue, who had been by my side through thick and thin since fifth grade. The one anchor I thought I had left was now pulled up and setting sail. I would greatly miss our regular chats.

My heart sunk. What will I do now? As tears streamed down my cheeks, I set my face like flint toward God in prayer and diligently asked, *Lord, send me a friend.*

Because I was housebound with an illness, this prayer felt nearly hopeless to me. Oftentimes, the voice of discouragement would chide me, saying, "How can you possibly meet anyone when you can't go out anywhere?"

Then one day my stepdaughter, who had no idea of my prayer or what I was going through, introduced me to her future mother-in-law. It didn't take long until we realized we had much in common. This started a chain of visits where we started studying the Bible together and watching our favorite videos.

Soon I started to develop my writing gift. I desired the companionship of another writer—I wanted someone to give feedback on ideas and help sort through issues. Scanning through an Internet writing site, I came across another devotional writer. As I read her author biography, I noticed we shared many common interests. I felt compelled to buy her book, and as I placed my order in an envelope, a thought crossed my mind: Why not send her a few writings of your own? So I did.

A few weeks later, her book arrived with a note thanking me for my writings and inviting me to e-mail her. I excitedly accepted the invitation and knew after our first conversation that we were kindred spirits. I felt this was confirmed when I looked up at the picture on the calendar hanging above me and I saw a huge daisy—part of her online name.

But God wasn't finished answering my prayer yet. My niece, with whom I had lost contact after my sister died, phoned me and started coming over for visits. Then, my husband's friend invited him to a new church. Shortly thereafter, the women in the congregation started reaching out to me.

Although I felt overwhelmed and discouraged over the loss of old friendships, God had a plan. I am thankful and enjoy each new friend He has brought into my path. As I realize the blessing of friendship, I find myself remaining open for God to send me a friend.

ACTION STEP

THINK OF ONE WAY YOU CAN AFFIRM ONE OF YOUR CLOSE FRIENDS. A LETTER. A SMALL GIFT. A SURPRISE TREAT. A PHONE CALL TO SAY, "I'M THINKING OF YOU." OPEN YOUR HEART TO A NEW FRIENDSHIP. SOMEONE NEEDS YOUR SUPPORT AND FRIENDSHIP IN THEIR LIFE.

PRAY FOR A FRIEND TODAY.

PRAYER

Thank You, heavenly Father, for my friends. Teach me to be a great friend to each of them. Lead me to someone who needs a friend.

FORGIVENESS

ONE OF THE TRUE TESTS OF FAITH AND PERHAPS THE MOST POWERFUL EXPRESSION OF LOVE IS WHEN WE FORGIVE OTHERS.

I can forgive, but I cannot forget, is only another way of saying, I will not forgive. Forgiveness ought to be like a cancelled note— torn in two, and burned up, so that it never can be shown against one.

HENRY WARD BEECHER

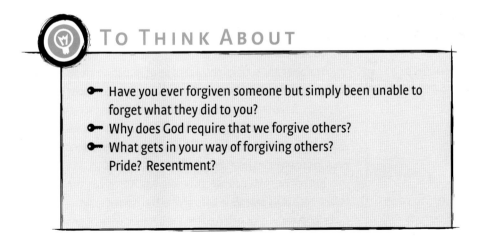

To Think About

- Have you ever forgiven someone but simply been unable to forget what they did to you?
- Why does God require that we forgive others?
- What gets in your way of forgiving others? Pride? Resentment?

LESSON FOR LIFE

Promises

God will:

Make you blameless
Colossians 1:22

Take sole responsibility
for vengeance
Romans 12:19

Forgive you as you
forgive others
Matthew 6:14-15

Forgive Us Our Debts

BIBLE STUDY PASSAGE: MATTHEW 18:21-35

Be kind and loving to each other, and forgive each other just as God forgave you in Christ.

EPHESIANS 4:32

Forgiveness is one of the most profound, pervasive, and powerful teachings within the Bible—but also one of the most difficult!

Are we required to forgive someone who abused us? An unfaithful spouse? A person who hurts our child? One who persistently takes advantage of us?

The clear and simple message of Jesus is that we are to forgive—anyone and always. In the Lord's Prayer, our model for prayer, Jesus teaches that it is only as we forgive others that forgiveness takes hold in our own life (Luke 6:37). He knows it will be difficult, but He reminds us that our love must extend even to our enemies (Matthew 5:44).

But not everyone deserves to be forgiven! This is very true. In fact, none of us deserve to be forgiven. This is what makes God's forgiveness of us so incredible and unexpected. As Paul said so eloquently, "When we were unable to help ourselves, at the moment of our need, Christ died for us, although we were living against God. Very few people will die to save the life of someone else. Although perhaps for a good person someone might possibly die. But God shows his great love for us in this way: Christ died for us while we were still sinners" (Romans 5:6-8).

Does this mean that the sin against me doesn't really matter? God never requires or asks us to minimize the pain and trauma of sin. God doesn't want us to be in denial as to what happened to us. And even after we forgive someone, it doesn't mean that all the earthly penalty is absolved. If someone has committed a crime, the legal system will still do its work.

Do I have to forget? Paul says that we aren't to remember and count someone's ways against them (1 Corinthians 13:5). That doesn't mean, however, we can just magically and instantly forget harsh and painful words or some other attack on us. But we do need to give even our memories to God and ask Him to bring healing over time.

What if I can't forgive? Again, present your situation and sorrow to God and trust that He is working in your life right now, even if the feelings aren't there.

You will have mercy on us again; you will conquer our sins. You will throw away all our sins into the deepest part of the sea.
Micah 7:19

REAL LIFE

Forgiveness or a Promissory Note?

JUDY HAMPTON

I have the capacity to harbor bitter memories. At one time they kept me in a prison of my own making.

Many years ago, my husband and I were separated. Young and naïve, we were disillusioned that life had not fulfilled our expectations. Although I was pregnant with our second child, my husband felt he needed a break. During our separation, he wrote me several long letters. He rationalized his decision to leave and his discontentment with life. However, his letters assured me, he still loved me. A few months before our beautiful daughter was born, we reconciled.

"I want to make our marriage work. I love you so much," my husband said. I wanted the same thing.

So we made every effort to change our lives. But we lacked the power within to bring about any permanent change.

Two years later, a friend shared the gospel with me, and I received Christ as my Lord and Savior. Immediately God began to transform my life. He gave me His power to love my husband and our children in a brand new way. My husband took notice, and within three months, he received Christ as his Savior as well. It was wonderful watching God resurrect this dead marriage. Our interactions were laced with a renewed grace and love.

Over and over my husband asked me to forgive him for the past. I assured him I had—but the truth is that I only said I had. In reality, I held onto my painful memories of the ways he had hurt me by taping all his letters to the bottom of my dresser drawer. I would reread them from time to time and rekindle the bitterness.

A couple of years later I attended a Christian women's club. I was riveted as the speaker shared that for many years she kept a mental list of all her husband's hurtful words against her.

She said, "One day God spoke to me through 1 Corinthians 13—'Love does not keep a record of wrongs.' It dawned on me that even though Christ had forgiven me of all my sins, I withheld forgiveness from my husband."

As soon as those words came out of the speaker's mouth, I felt tremendous conviction in my soul.

Oh God, I have kept a promissory note on my husband instead of totally forgiving him. I've wanted him to earn back my love, yet You don't ask that of me. I am so ashamed, I prayed silently.

After the luncheon, I sped home to retrieve those letters. I lit a fire in the fireplace and tossed each one into the flames. As each letter turned to ashes, my heart melted. I wept in repentance over my own sin and that day I forgave my husband. The Lord showed me in that moment that I don't have a righteous life—I have a forgiven life.

ACTION STEP

IF YOU ARE STRUGGLING TO FORGIVE SOMEONE, THERE MAY NOT BE AN IMME-DIATE, SINGULAR MOMENT WHEN THE ISSUE IS RESOLVED FOR YOU. THERE CAN BE A SINGLE MOMENT, HOWEVER, WHEN WE COMMIT TO FORGIVING ANOTHER. ARE YOU READY? WITH GOD'S HELP, WILL YOU DO THAT TODAY?

PRAYER

Beyond my feelings, I extend to others the same forgiveness You lavished on me.

A NEW HEART

GOD'S MIRACULOUS POWER CAN OVERCOME A LIFETIME OF CONDITIONING, BAD CHOICES, AND STUBBORNNESS TO CREATE A NEW HEART.

None but God can satisfy the longings of an immortal soul;
that as the heart was made for Him, so He only can fill it.

RICHARD CHENEVIX TRENCH

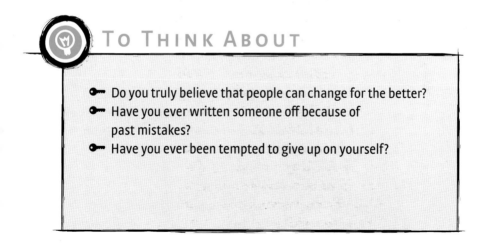

TO THINK ABOUT

- Do you truly believe that people can change for the better?
- Have you ever written someone off because of past mistakes?
- Have you ever been tempted to give up on yourself?

LESSON FOR LIFE

Promises

God will:

Forgive sins and give His presence

Acts 3:19

Give you understanding

Romans 12:2

Renew your inner being

Colossians 3:10

Continue to work on you

Philippians 1:6

Do We Really Have a Choice?

BIBLE STUDY PASSAGE: LUKE 19:2-8

If anyone belongs to Christ, there is a new creation. The old things have gone; everything is made new!

2 CORINTHIANS 5:17

There are several forms of determinism prevalent in the fields of education and psychology today. One is a causal determinism, the belief that everything a person does is determined by the shaping influences in their lives like parents and life experiences. Common expressions would include sayings like, "Once a person is five, their personality is shaped and you can't really change it."

A more popular kind of determinism says that we are primarily a psychological product of genetics, so our behavior and attitudes follow from the way we are "wired." Common expressions of this would include: "I can't help it, it's just the way I was born"; or "a leopard can't change his spots"; or "the nut doesn't fall far from the tree."

Though nature and nurture have a huge impact on us as persons, aren't you glad that there is a miraculous, powerful

God who is able to change even the most stubborn, damaged, sinful heart? Paul goes so far as to say, "Therefore, if anyone is in Christ, he is a new creation" (2 Corinthians 5:17 NKJV). After a change of heart at the moment of conversion, God isn't finished with us, either. Paul says: "We all show the Lord's glory, and we are being changed to be like him. This change in us brings ever greater glory, which comes from the Lord, who is the Spirit" (2 Corinthians 3:18).

But you don't understand my upbringing. You don't understand mistakes I've made. You don't understand how hard it is for me to break certain negative patterns.

With grace, with faith, with the help of godly friends, you can say along with Paul: "I keep trying to reach the goal and get the prize for which God called me through Christ to the life above" (Philippians 3:14). Because of His forgiving, life-changing power, God's ultimate concern with your life is not where you've been but where you are going.

You have left your old sinful life and the things you did before. You have begun to live the new life, in which you are being made new and are becoming like the One who made you.

Colossians 3:9-10

REAL LIFE

From Mother-in-Law to Mother-in-Love

KAREN R. KILBY

It had been a difficult relationship, almost non-existent—my mother-in-law's drinking problem stood in the way of us having a normal one.

As my husband and I began to raise our family, this became more and more of a concern. However, now my husband David was having a change of heart, telling me he wanted to offer his dad a job, of all things. He would fly back to his parents' home in Michigan, pack up their belongings, and drive them to our home in Florida. And even worse, they would live with us for six weeks while the condo they had purchased was being renovated! What a turn of events! We had been relieved to have the distance between us when we moved to Florida five years before. What in the world had happened to change David's mind?

Ever since David had turned his life over to God, I had seen positive changes taking place. He was becoming more tenderhearted. It was evident in how David interacted with me and with the children, which I loved, but this decision was something I was finding very difficult to accept. How would I live with an alcoholic—even if only for six weeks? I knew David had made up his mind, and so I prayed and prayed again in desperation. *I don't want to do this, Lord—help me to be willing! I'll open my home, but You will have to open my heart.*

When David's parents arrived, it was as though they sensed and respected my unspoken request. Even though at times they were at odds with each other, they seemed to enjoy being with us. Gradually, we began to see changes taking place between them, especially changes in my mother-in-law. She had an aura of peace about her that had not been there before. She seemed to be more relaxed and enjoying life, greeting me each morning with a smile. We could actually enjoy each other's company—going to lunch together, shopping together, and planning meals together. As we visited, we became friends for the first time.

Soon, I began to learn the reason for the changes I saw—the result of a changed heart. Just before David had offered his dad a job, his mother had fallen and broken her hip. While she recovered in the hospital, one of the nurses discovered she liked to read and gave her *The Hiding Place* by Corrie Ten Boom. As she read the book, my mother-in-law found her own hiding place as she realized and accepted God's love for herself.

A strong and loving friendship developed between us as we shared our God-centered common interests. She became not my mother-in-law but my mother-in-love.

ACTION STEP

IDENTIFY A NEW ATTITUDE OR A NEW HABIT YOU WANT TO GROW AND
BLOSSOM IN YOUR LIFE. OR, IDENTIFY AN OLD ATTITUDE OR AN OLD HABIT YOU
WANT ELIMINATED FROM YOUR LIFE. COMMIT THIS CHANGE OF HEART TO
GOD AND ASK HIM TO DO A SPECIAL WORK IN YOU. YOU MIGHT EXPERIENCE
AN INSTANTANEOUS, MIRACULOUS CHANGE—OR YOU MIGHT EXPERIENCE A
GRADUAL GROWTH AND GRACE. EITHER WAY, YOUR CHALLENGE IS NOT TO TRY
HARDER, BUT TO TRUST MORE.

PRAYER

*Thank You, O God, for making me a new person through Your Son Jesus. I ask
You to continue and complete the good work You started in me.*

SELF-IMAGE

YOUR ABILITY TO EXPRESS LOVE TO OTHERS IS LINKED TO YOUR ABILITY TO LOVE YOURSELF.

The value of a person is not measured on an applause meter;
it is measured in the heart and mind of God.

JOHN FISCHER

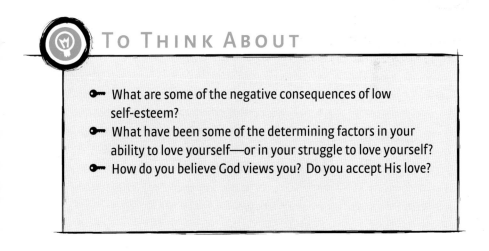

TO THINK ABOUT

- What are some of the negative consequences of low self-esteem?
- What have been some of the determining factors in your ability to love yourself—or in your struggle to love yourself?
- How do you believe God views you? Do you accept His love?

LESSON FOR LIFE

Promises	# The Woman at the Well
	BIBLE STUDY PASSAGE: 4:4-26
God will:	

The Lord did not care for you and choose you because there were many of you—you are the smallest nation of all. But the Lord chose you because he loved you, and he kept his promise to your ancestors.

DEUTERONOMY 7:7-8

Promises

God will:

Honor your kindness
Proverbs 19:22

Honor your inner beauty
1 Timothy 2:10
Proverbs 31:30

Accept you and
justify you
Romans 3:30

Love you as a mother
loves her baby
Isaiah 49:15

If ever there was a person who had reasons to struggle with their self-image, it was the woman who met Jesus at the well as recorded in John 4.

• *First of all, she was a Samaritan. In Jesus' day, the Jews despised all Samaritans as religious infidels and "half breeds." When Israel was conquered by the Babylonians in 586 B.C., the youngest and most educated were taken into captivity. When their descendants returned to Jerusalem seventy years later, they expected to find a thriving center of worship and faith. Instead, many who had been left behind converted to other religions and married people from other countries. They were despised from that moment on.*
• *Second, she was a woman, which meant she had second-class status*

in her culture and was viewed as the "property" of her husband.

• Third, she had failed at love. Jesus asked her where her husband was. She admitted she wasn't married, but was living with a man. Jesus pointed out she had previously been married six times! Whether a serial widow or divorcee, she had probably given up on marital vows.

• Fourth, she was rejected by her peers. Jesus met her during the hottest time of the day with no one else around her. The women of Middle East villages gathered water at the well together *during the coolest part of the day.*

But when Jesus entered her life, everything changed. He took the initiative and spoke to her first, uncommon for a man to do in that culture. In the same way, He reaches out to us long before we reach toward Him. He looked at her as a person on the basis of her potential—not her past or even her present circumstances. Most importantly, He offered her a living water that would satisfy the emptiness and longing of her soul, a drink of water that would provide renewal for her parched soul and life.

Even if you feel as needy as a lonely Samaritan at a well today, be assured that Jesus provides you with all the reasons you need to love and embrace yourself.

So the King will greatly desire your beauty; because He is your Lord, worship Him.
Psalm 45:11 NKJV

REAL LIFE

A Very Special Young Lady

NANCY B. GIBBS

During my childhood years, I had low self-esteem. Saying I wasn't fond of school is an understatement. Actually, I hated school. Every afternoon, I watched the clock waiting for the dismissal bell to ring. My grades reflected my low self-esteem—I had no desire to learn.

I had been a worrier my entire life. My father said many times that my first sentence was "I'm worried." For some reason, my intense worries kept me from being able to perform well in school or any other aspect of my life. As a result, I never saw myself as anyone worthwhile.

It seemed the older I got, the further behind I became. I was quiet, shy, and withdrawn. Very few people knew me. How could I expect anyone to understand me? I didn't even understand myself. I never felt like I did anything in an extraordinary way. I didn't have the desire to go to college—I didn't really have any interests I wanted to pursue.

I did have one ambition: When someone asked me what I wanted to become as an adult, my response was always, "A mother."

Little changed as I entered my teen years. I simply wanted to blend in with the crowd. I didn't want to be noticed. By the grace of God, I graduated from high school and married at an early age.

I was delighted when I discovered that I was expecting a child. I loved the thought of becoming a mother. Many of the students who attended high school with me were getting ready to go off to college. I was getting ready for what I anticipated would be the greatest day of my life.

God not only blessed me with one baby boy; He gave me two. Two nurses walked into my room the next morning, each holding a baby. I was too weak to hold both babies at one time, so one of the nurses stayed with me. I looked into my babies' tiny faces and rejoiced. I felt like I had done something right for the first time in my life.

In the quietness of the moment as I met my two little boys, the nurse smiled a warm and sensitive smile. "God must think you are a very special mother, honey, to have given you two babies at one time," she whispered.

"Who, me?" I inquired. "Special?"

"Yes, you," she said. "You must be a very special young lady." The nurse saw me as a special mother. God obviously saw me as His princess—a person worthy of His blessings.

To this day, some thirty-one years later, I remember how important I felt the day that God blessed me so richly. Even though I never saw myself as anyone special, God saw me as His child worthy of abundant blessings and His love. He made me a mother—and a very special mother indeed!

ACTION STEP

You've written letters to others as a way to affirm your love for and belief in them. Write a letter to yourself, reminding you of how much God loves you—and your own sense of self appreciation. Tuck it anywhere you can read it as a reminder of this soul matter.

PRAYER

Thank You, God, for being the One who believes in me and loves me as no one else ever could. You see in my heart and declare me beautiful.

HONESTY

TELLING THE TRUTH IS FOUNDATIONAL TO RELATIONSHIPS AND A CLEAR CONSCIENCE.

*Those who think it is permissible
to tell white lies soon grow color-blind.*

AUSTIN O'MALLEY

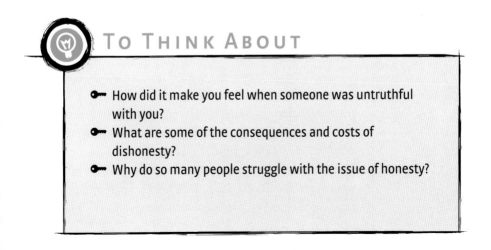

TO THINK ABOUT

- 🔑 How did it make you feel when someone was untruthful with you?
- 🔑 What are some of the consequences and costs of dishonesty?
- 🔑 Why do so many people struggle with the issue of honesty?

LESSON FOR LIFE

Promises

God Will:

Perfect your character
James 1:4

Reward your honest
efforts
Job 34:11

Cause you to shine
Philippians 2:15

Bring peace to the
honest
Psalm 37:37

Set Apart

BIBLE STUDY PASSAGE: PSALM 24:3-6

Do not let anyone treat you as if you are unimportant because you are young. Instead, be an example to the believers with your words, your actions, your love, your faith, and your pure life.

1 TIMOTHY 4:12

Paul wrote two letters to his young protégé, Timothy, giving special attention to Timothy's integrity. He wanted him to exhibit a blameless, godly lifestyle of purity through his words and actions.

Paul's biggest concern for this young pastor and the young church was expressed when he said: "But if I am delayed, I write so that you may know how you ought to conduct yourself in the house of God, which is the church of the living God, the pillar and ground of the truth" (1 Timothy 3:15 NKJV). As the Christian church grew and made headway in an immoral (or amoral) and permissive culture, there were a myriad of questions raised by new believers about ethics and truth.

Though Paul recognized that there can be legitimate disagreements on matters of conscience, one non-negotiable was that followers of Jesus Christ should have the highest standard of honesty.

Even in the church in Jerusalem, where it was expected that members came from a more honest and moral society, lying was a problem and was judged with severity. (See the story of Ananias and Sapphira in Acts 5.)

We, too, live in a permissive society that does not always show high regard for telling the truth. We have the same opportunity as Timothy and the early Christian church to make a profound impact on others through our honesty. Paul expressed this prayer for another first-century church: "that you may become blameless and harmless, children of God without fault in the midst of a crooked and perverse generation, among whom you shine as lights in the world" (Philippians 2:15 NKJV).

The Lord doesn't like it when we cheat in business.
Proverbs 16:11 CEV

REAL LIFE

A Little Honesty Goes a Long Way

KATHRYN LAY

Even though my earthly father didn't believe that a few cents' dishonesty was a problem in the grand scheme of life, I knew that my heavenly Father valued honesty in His children, and that's probably why I prayed for ways to pass that idea along to my daughter.

That opportunity came when we were on our first real vacation as a family and our daughter was only six. While going through the shops in the square of a small, country town, I found a handmade candle that I couldn't resist. We left the shop with our new purchase and wandered in and out of other stores for half an hour until we came to a café and stopped for lunch.

As we ate and relaxed, a young woman walked into the shop and looked around. She spotted us and hurried to our table. I was puzzled, then recognized her as the clerk who had waited on us in the candle shop.

She held out a dollar bill to me as if it were mine.

"What's this?" I asked, a little embarrassed that others were looking at us.

"I'm sorry, but I overcharged you for the candle," she explained. "I've been looking in all the shops trying to find you. I was afraid you had already left town, but since it's lunchtime, I thought you might be here."

I was shocked to learn how much time she'd spent searching for us. Had she closed the shop or had to wait for someone to take her place while she searched? I never would have known, or even cared, about the slight over-charge. In fact, I told her that very thing.

She said, "Oh, but it doesn't matter the amount—the mistake was mine. I needed to find you." She smiled and I knew that the honesty in her soul had been tested, and she was happy.

I noticed after that trip that whenever my daughter and I stood in line and someone dropped some change, Michelle would pick it up and give it to them. Even when she didn't know who had lost the dime in the post office or the quarter at the Laundromat, she walked around asking, "Does this belong to you?"

Like most children, she loved finding loose change and declaring, "Mine!" But now, she is determined to find the real owners and keep her own soul honest. A stranger's honesty and determination to follow through with the importance of returning one dollar, even at her own inconvenience, had somehow changed my daughter's way of thinking about her values.

I don't know if this young woman remembered the event as strongly as I have, but I know God uses such moments to change our lives. And every time Michelle places a penny in a stranger's hand and they smile at her in surprise, I wonder if they too will remember that small, honest moment.

ACTION STEP

MARK TWAIN GAVE ONE REASON THAT IT IS ALWAYS IMPORTANT TO TELL THE TRUTH: "IF YOU TELL THE TRUTH YOU DON'T HAVE TO REMEMBER ANYTHING." ONLY LIARS HAVE TO KEEP THEIR STORY "STRAIGHT." IF YOU'VE BEEN UNTRUTHFUL WITH SOMEONE, FIND YOUR COURAGE, APPROACH THEM, APOLOGIZE, AND CORRECT YOUR DISHONESTY.

PRAYER

You, Lord, are the Author of the truth and light. Help me to reflect Your purity in my words.

A MOTHER'S LOVE

LOVING OUR CHILDREN IS ONE OF THE CLEAREST WAYS WE BECOME MORE LIKE JESUS.

Making the decision to have a child is momentous. It is to decide forever to have your heart go walking around outside your body.

ELIZABETH STONE

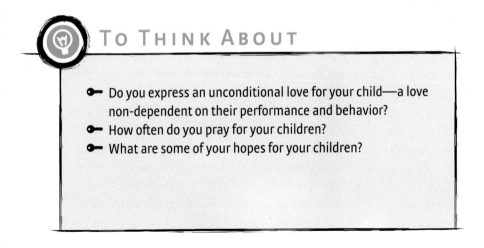

TO THINK ABOUT

- Do you express an unconditional love for your child—a love non-dependent on their performance and behavior?
- How often do you pray for your children?
- What are some of your hopes for your children?

LESSON FOR LIFE

Promises

God Will:

Help you accomplish
good things
2 Corinthians 9:8

Strengthen you
Philippians 4:13

Use trials to perfect your
character
Romans 5:3

Comfort you
Psalm 147:3

Blessings of a Mother

BIBLE STUDY PASSAGE: LUKE 1:42-55

But we were very gentle with you, like a mother caring for her little children. Because we loved you, we were happy to share not only God's Good News with you, but even our own lives. You had become so dear to us!

1 THESSALONIANS 2:7-8

When Paul wrote his letter to the Greek church in Thessalonica, he could think of no greater way to describe his love for the people than to compare it to the love a mother has for her children. Not only was he gentle as their leader, but he loved them so much he poured his very life into them. What better description of a mother's love is there?

All who birthed a child understand full well that there are challenges to being a parent. Children can be difficult and needy. No wonder Paul considers the greatest character trait of a Christian to be love, and goes on to describe it terms and phrases like *kindness, not self serving, not easily angered, always protects,* and *always hopes* (see 1 Corinthians 13).

In some cases, children are difficult because they are needy and fragile. The good news is that God bestows special strength and comfort to those who comfort others—like the mother who comforts her child. (See 2 Corinthians 1:2-5.)

But at the end of the day, as you pour your life into your children, know that a special blessing from God awaits you. May you hear in your heart what was said of Jesus' mother: "Blessed is the mother who gave you birth and nursed you" (Luke 11:27 NKJV).

Standing near his cross were Jesus' mother, his mother's sister, Mary the wife of Clopas, and Mary Magdalene. When Jesus saw his mother and the follower he loved standing nearby, he said to his mother, "Dear woman, here is your son." Then he said to the follower, "Here is your mother." From that time on, the follower took her to live in his home.
John 19:25-27

 REAL LIFE

The Love of a Son

LOUISE TUCKER JONES

I hung up the telephone with a sigh of relief. My son's speech pathologist was running fifteen minutes late, giving me some much-needed time to get myself ready and help Jay, my nineteen-year-old son with Down syndrome. We finally made it into the bathroom to brush his teeth when suddenly, the color drained from his face and he fell into my arms, unconscious. In an instant my day went from "almost normal" to a slow-motion, adrenaline-pumping emergency.

As I called 911, my heart pounded and I could hear the fear in my own voice as I quickly exclaimed, "My son has severe heart disease and has just passed out!" As I knelt beside my son, the cardiologist's words hammered in my memory. "Jay is at great risk for a stroke or fatal cardiac arrhythmia." My hands shook as I bathed his pale face with a wet cloth and prayed silently, *Please God, don't let him die!*

Just a few minutes earlier, I was making plans to meet my husband for lunch while Jay spent a couple of hours with his speech pathologist. Now my mind was deluged with thoughts like, "We didn't make it to the twentieth birthday after all." This was to be his "miracle birthday," the birthday that doctors had never given us hope of seeing. The big party was only two weeks away. Now here we were, paramedics rushing in trying to save my child.

I stepped away as trained hands immediately went to work taking blood pressure, pulse, and oxygen saturation levels. An eternity seemed to pass. Finally, some color began to creep into Jay's face and he was coherent enough to answer questions.

Finally it was determined that Jay had had a "vasovagal" response to hitting his knee earlier, causing him to faint when he stood up too quickly with severe pain. No stroke. No fatal cardiac arrhythmia. No speeding ambulance rushing us to the hospital. We would see that twentieth birthday.

Being the mother of a medically fragile child, this scene was all too familiar, certainly not my first brush with a life-threatening emergency. Each time a crisis passed, I tried to push the fear away from my consciousness. But just like a jack-in-the-box, wound up and ready to pop, that fear would lunge to the fore-front with each subsequent crisis.

But in spite of his health problems, this precious son of mine is filled with joy, laughter, song, and unconditional love. And if God suddenly leaned down from the heavens and whispered in my ear, "Louise, if you had known from the beginning how difficult this road was going to be, would you have chosen to walk it?" I can say without a doubt that my answer would be, "Yes!" With all of my heart and soul I would walk every step of this journey, just for the love of my son.

ACTION STEP

WHAT IS ONE SIMPLE, TANGIBLE THING YOU DO WITH YOUR CHILDREN THAT
SHOWS THEM HOW MUCH YOU REALLY LOVE THEM? IF POSSIBLE, FIND A TIME
TO DO THAT IN THE NEXT TWENTY-FOUR HOURS.

PRAYER

*O God, don't let me ever take for granted the blessing you have given me in my
children. Grant me the strength and peace to build a love for You in their lives.*

FREEDOM FROM PERFECTIONISM

WE MUST CULTIVATE A SPIRIT OF APPRECIATION OVER JUDGMENTALISM IF WE ARE TO AFFIRM THE PEOPLE IN OUR LIVES—AND AFFIRM OURSELVES.

American women expect to find in their husbands a perfection that English women only hope to find in their butlers.

SOMERSET MAUGHAM

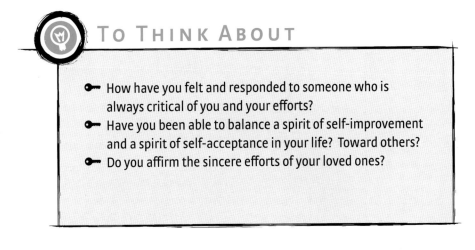

TO THINK ABOUT

- How have you felt and responded to someone who is always critical of you and your efforts?
- Have you been able to balance a spirit of self-improvement and a spirit of self-acceptance in your life? Toward others?
- Do you affirm the sincere efforts of your loved ones?

LESSON FOR LIFE

Promises

God will:

Produce fruit in your life

Galatians 5:22

Give grace

Hebrews 4:16

Use you to reveal Christ

2 Corinthians 2:14

Use you to build up

believers

Ephesians 4:15-16

Humble and Patient

BIBLE STUDY PASSAGE: EPHESIANS 4:1-16

Christ accepted you, so you should accept each other, which will bring glory to God.

ROMANS 15:7

When Paul wrote the letter to the church in Ephesus, he was very concerned that Christian believers understand their "exalted" new position through grace—"blessed in the heavenly realms with every spiritual blessing in Christ" (1:3 NKJV)—and then how that grace is to be lived out among our spiritual friends and family members.

Beginning in chapter 4, he challenges these young people of faith to "live a life worthy" of God's grace and calling (4:1 NKJV) by the way they treat each other. In verses 2 and 3 he spells this out: We love each other through humility, gentleness, patience, bearing one another in love, and by committing ourselves to unity.

What a contrast to the critical and cynical age in which we live, where tearing others down is considered a fun sport. What a contrast to the messages that many of us have received and accepted since early childhood that only the very best from ourselves and others is satisfactory. What a contrast to a slate of self-help titles at the bookstore that preach the necessity of perfect bodies, perfect relationships, and perfect kids. We too easily run after perfection and forget to love!

- Humility keeps us from the sin of arrogance and from looking down on others—both major relationship killers.
- Gentleness means we speak and act in ways that don't hurt others but that build others up.
- Patience demonstrates that we truly believe God can and is working in another person's life—even if we want more progress right now!
- Bearing one another means that we love someone even when he or she is difficult.
- Keeping unity means we are wise enough to know how much we really do need each other.

Perfectionism can reflect a magnificent desire to think, speak, and act in the highest forms possible. Wonderful! As long as we continue to honor others, ourselves, and God through the qualities of humility, gentleness, patience, and unity!

> When you talk, do not say harmful things, but say what people need— words that will help others become stronger. Then what you say will do good to those who listen to you.
>
> Ephesians 4:29

REAL LIFE

When Perfectionism Causes Great Pains

KATHY COLLARD MILLER

I walked into our home and almost bumped into my husband, Larry, who was grinning like a Cheshire cat.

What is he up to? I wondered.

He said, "Come into the kitchen." I followed him and with a flourish of his hand, he pointed to the dish-less sink. "I did the dishes for you!" He stood there as if he'd just accepted the Nobel Peace Prize.

"Wow!" I breathed. Larry rarely did the dishes—and then only when I asked. Yet, he had done them this time without me even asking! I was so excited. I wrapped my arms around him for a hug, but as I looked over his shoulder, pieces of food and puddles of milk curdling on the kitchen counter leered at me. He didn't wipe off the counter! Anyone knows you haven't finished the dishes until you wipe off the counter!

Just as I began to open my mouth to instruct him in proper dishwashing, I remembered that I'd been working on releasing my perfectionistic expectations. I'd recently identified myself as a perfectionist, and one of the characteristics of that emotional hang-up is not giving credit or praise unless something is done perfectly. Or, as someone has quipped, "A perfectionist is a person who takes great pains and passes them on to others."

I'd done my share of "passing" over the years, so I was trying to let God help me in that area. Here was my chance. I could give Larry credit even though he hadn't completed the task perfectly—like I would. Plus, had I ever let him know that doing the dishes includes wiping off the kitchen counter? I'd been taught that as a child, but obviously he hadn't. It wasn't really fair to expect him to read my mind or know instinctively what I'd been taught. No, he hadn't done a perfect job, but he had done an excellent job—the best he knew how.

As my mind clarified over these truths, I knew what I should do. Instead of commenting on what he hadn't done, I praised him for what he had done. "Honey," I exclaimed, "Thanks so much for supporting me in this way!"

I was so glad I bit my tongue and appreciated his loving gift—even if it wasn't done perfectly. And, guess what? Larry did the dishes again the next evening! I bet he wouldn't have done them again—and many times since then—if I'd criticized his efforts. Of course, there's often the need for us to instruct someone about how to do something better, but I've learned to do it not in their moment of glory but later, when it won't be poorly received.

By appreciating excellence instead of demanding perfection for several years now, of both myself and others, I've found that even though my perfectionism is not cured, it is currently in remission.

ACTION STEP

KEEP A NOTE CARD WITH YOU THROUGHOUT THE DAY. DRAW A LINE DOWN THE MIDDLE AND PUT TWO HEADERS: BUILDING UP AND CRITICIZING.

NOW KEEP A TALLY OF YOUR COMMUNICATION TO OTHERS. BE HONEST WITH YOURSELF. DO YOU TRULY BUILD OTHERS UP? IF YOU DON'T LIKE THE ANSWER, WHAT CAN YOU DO ABOUT IT?

PRAYER

Help me, O kind and gracious God, to extend to others the same mercy You extend to me.

WHEN IT'S HARD TO LOVE

LOVE IS MUCH MORE THAN A ROMANTIC FEELING—SOMETIMES IT IS JUST PLAIN HARD WORK.

The art of love is largely the art of persistence.

ALBERT ELLIS

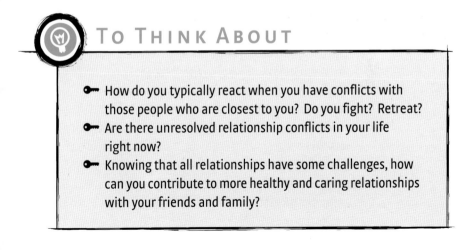

TO THINK ABOUT

- How do you typically react when you have conflicts with those people who are closest to you? Do you fight? Retreat?
- Are there unresolved relationship conflicts in your life right now?
- Knowing that all relationships have some challenges, how can you contribute to more healthy and caring relationships with your friends and family?

LESSON FOR LIFE

Promises

God Will:

Perfect his love in you
1 John 4:12

Never stop loving you
Romans 8:39

Help you obey Him
John 15:4-5

Bless your efforts
Galatians 6:9

The Way Love Grows

BIBLE STUDY PASSAGE: GALATIANS 6:1-10

We must not become tired of doing good. We will receive our harvest of eternal life at the right time if we do not give up.

GALATIANS 6:9

In the sixth chapter of Galatians, Paul sets out some of the most practical principles for expressing love for one another found anywhere in the Bible. But just because they are practical doesn't make them easy!

First, he tells us that we should be redemptive people, helping restore those who have been caught in a sin (v. 1). He does caution you that as you reach out to help someone, be extra careful not to get trapped in sin yourself.

Secondly, Paul challenges us to love others unconditionally, without judgment and comparisons (v. 4). Competition can be friendly and healthy, but when it consumes our relationships, the inevitable result is conflict. How many marital and sibling relationships have been torpedoed by a spirit of striving rather than a spirit of pulling together?

Next, Paul urges us to help carry the "excessive weights" that others are forced to bear (v. 2). He does point out that each of us should carry our own "backpacks," so we aren't required to do everything for others (v. 5). But when someone has burdens that are bigger than any one person should handle alone, we are to step in help.

Most importantly, Paul reminds us not to give up on loving others (v. 9). Sure, some people are unbelievably difficult to love, but if we don't lose faith in God's power to authentically change their lives, our steadfast persistence may be the very thing that makes the difference between them finding God's forgiveness and peace or never receiving God's grace in their hearts.

The result of how we relate to others is simple, according to Paul. He says, "People harvest only what they plant" (v. 7). When we sow love into others, we will ultimately receive love in return.

Love will cover a multitude of sins.

1 Peter 4:8 NKJV

REAL LIFE

Follow Through

LYNDA BLAIR VERNALIA

I am sitting on a hotel bed, fuming, the starlight outside doing nothing to placate my mood. I have not planned on leaving, but the options seem limited.

"Well, if you hate me so much, divorce me!" I had yelled, exiting with a slam.

"Sounds like the usual plan!" I heard him scream through the paneling.

Eyes flashing white, I shoved some clothes in a bag and checked in to the nearest hotel.

Flopping lengthwise across the king-size bed, I ponder, Why do our fights always end the same? I push him away; he lets me go. We muddle through these wonderful absolutes: "always" and "never." Will we ever break this cycle? I trace back my frustration, reliving my father endlessly berating me as a little girl.

"You're so sensitive! Can't you lighten up?"

Throughout my marriage I have endeavored to let go of anger, to forgive quickly, to apologize. I was determined we would not become our divorced parents. But this is the proverbial "it." I ask myself if I really have to follow through.

So, now what? I mull over belongings and assets. Where could I go? Dad's? School? Go back to being alone, to a dating scene I hardly ever knew? Do the last five years just become a memory?

Of course, living alone is cheaper—probably cleaner, too. I have a good-paying job; I could start a PhD. I will not remarry; I will just have a string of lovers at my beck and call. Fettuccine and Tuscan wine every night! Check the other whine at the door! Who says I have to change?

I quiet myself, brushing lonely brown tangles from my mouth.

"I'll never have a baby," I whisper. I have waited five years for "the right time." But there has "never" been enough money or enough space. I crave motherhood, to share the good that I know. Hmmm—maybe it is time to commit to someone besides myself.

Outside my mind, the telephone buzzes. The front desk requests permission to allow someone upstairs. My husband takes the receiver and my frost starts to melt. I am who I want to be again: a family member.

As he rides the elevator to apologize, I am grateful he understands that tonight I need a rescue; with practice, I will not tomorrow.

Love takes more fine tuning then learning to play the clarinet (and that took me at least five years to play with some semblance of quality!). God gave me my husband and together we shape what love means. For us it is forgiveness; tonight, it works. I treasure these words from our wedding prayer: We ask for words both kind and gentle and hearts ready and willing to ask for forgiveness as well as to forgive. Lord, we put our marriage into your hands.

My husband knocks. Now, our family can follow through—and forgive.

Since that night, we have journeyed on with daily forgiveness and daily determination to love each other, sometimes stumbling along the way. And there have been no more evenings spent in lonely hotel rooms.

 ## ACTION STEP

- WHAT PERSON IN YOUR LIFE IS CARRYING A PARTICULARLY HEAVY BURDEN? WHAT IS ONE THING YOU CAN DO TO LIGHTEN THEIR LOAD?
- WHO IS ONE PERSON WHO HAS DRIFTED AWAY FROM GOD AND FALLEN INTO A SINFUL LIFESTYLE? HOW CAN GOD USE YOU TO GENTLY RESTORE THAT PERSON?

 ## PRAYER

Thank You for the love, joy, and peace You have brought into my life, O God— help me to extend those same qualities of grace to others.

TRUSTING GOD

THE BEST WAY TO FACE DOUBTS AND FEAR IS THROUGH ACKNOWLEDGING GOD WHO IS FAITHFUL AND KIND.

Prayer crowns God with the honor and glory due His name,
and God crowns prayer with assurance and comfort.
The most praying souls are the most assured souls.

THOMAS BENTON BROOKS

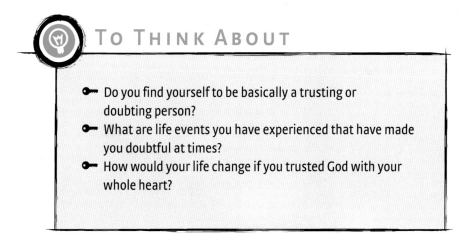

TO THINK ABOUT

- ⚷ Do you find yourself to be basically a trusting or doubting person?
- ⚷ What are life events you have experienced that have made you doubtful at times?
- ⚷ How would your life change if you trusted God with your whole heart?

LESSON FOR LIFE

Promises

God will:

Hear your prayers
2 Chronicles 7:14
Psalm 16:1-2

Be near you
Psalm 145:18

Console you
Jeremiah 31:9

Be available to help you
Ephesians 2:18

Daily Dependence

BIBLE STUDY PASSAGE: PSALM 40

Trust the Lord with all your heart, and don't depend on your own understanding. Remember the Lord in all you do, and he will give you success.

PROVERBS 3:5-6

We rightfully teach our children—and attempt to live our own lives—by the credos of responsibility, self-control, and mature self-reliance.

And yes, being responsible is a very good thing. But when our attitude reaches the point where we trust more in ourselves than in God, twin temptations, both that lead to spiritual shipwreck, suddenly confront us.

One temptation is pride, an unhealthy arrogance that slips (or roars) into our thinking when things are going great in our lives. We become convinced that we are in control of our own world.

The second temptation, despair, works itself into our hearts when we face the inevitable difficulties and setbacks of life that are outside of our control—illness, a difficult relationship, an economic downturn.

Daily trusting in God—acknowledging that He is the one source of all good gifts and success and the only safe refuge when life is difficult—steers us from the twin dangers of pride and despair.

James points out that trials test and prove our faith (James 1:1-3), but we don't have to wait for challenging moments to begin trusting God with our entire life. The good news is that with complete and total trust in Him, He directs our steps in the most fulfilling paths for our lives.

> The Lord has heard my cry for help; the Lord will answer my prayer.
> Psalm 6:9

REAL LIFE

Crutches One Day, Wings the Next

LAURIE KLEIN

They were sending me on to experts. In my backlit X-rays, the tumor shone, cameo-pale, pinned deep in my shinbone. People lose legs to cancer.

Slumped in a lawn chair, I remembered losing our willow tree, the rot at its core expanding, encroaching on bark. Lightning had felled it in one stroke. Limbs splintered. The trunk oozed sap, a slow hemorrhage in the wet grass.

Above me a wedge of geese rose, tilted, and veered south. *Some bright morning,* I thought, humming the old hymn, *when this life is o'er, I'll fly away.*

Days passed. Friends entreated the God of Adam, for in His hands, miraculous life once bloomed from a single bone, divinely extracted. Post-Eden, had Adam suffered phantom pain? I was already battling RSD, a disease short-circuiting my nervous system, and daily, searing foot pain would likely worsen and spread after biopsy.

Before praying for me, our pastor spoke about Jairus, a man who beseeched Jesus to heal his daughter. Messengers had reported her dead before Jesus could reach her.

"Don't listen to them," the Savior said. "Just trust Me."

The morning my husband, Will, and I left for the dreaded appointment, I woke to a whispered thought in my spirit: *This is not about you—it's about My glory.*

Driving across state under migrating geese, we sensed a hundred prayers lifting us, and the miles sped by. While threading through Seattle traffic, a poem about a veteran came to mind. Rather than bemoan his lost leg, he resolved to live with twice the passion. Could I?

At the University Medical Center, I hobbled through Oncology where gaunt patients clutched paper cups mounded with ice chips.

Will took my crutches. "Just trust Him," he murmured.

We perched on plastic chairs in the specialist's office. Although smaller than a soap bubble, my tumor seemed to weigh a ton. Shifting my leg, I pictured the prayers of friends winging upward in unison, collectively bearing us toward our Father in heaven. When the doctor entered, I barely breathed.

"Enchondroma," he said, tapping my X-rays. "Calcified cartilage due to genetic defect."

"Is that bad?"

He leaned forward, translating. "It's benign."

"Benign," I repeated, several times, like someone just learning the language. No biopsy then. In that moment, Bill and I felt like orphanage kids on Christmas morn: Braced for something educational, we'd found a shiny red bike instead.

Later, we blew soap bubbles from our hotel balcony. A passing cyclist and several pedestrians halted below. "We're celebrating," I called. "My tumor's benign!"

Perfect strangers waved and cheered.

"Truly, in our own hearts we believed we would die," 2 Corinthians reads. "But this happened so we would not trust in ourselves but in God, who raises people from the dead."

ACTION STEP

THOUGH PEOPLE MAY LET US DOWN, GOD WILL NEVER FAIL US. ONE OF THE GREATEST WAYS TO EXPRESS OUR TRUST IN AND PRAISE FOR GOD IS THROUGH MUSIC. IF YOU ALREADY LISTEN TO PRAISE AND WORSHIP SONGS, PUT IN A FAVORITE CD AND SING YOUR HEART TO GOD. IF YOU DON'T HAVE ANY CHRISTIAN MUSIC IN THE HOUSE, VISIT A CHRISTIAN BOOKSTORE OR THE GOSPEL SECTION OF YOUR FAVORITE MEDIA OUTLET, AND SELECT SOMETHING THAT WILL REMIND YOU OF GOD'S GOODNESS.

PRAYER

Lord God, You are good. Thank You that You care for me. Help me spend today thanking You and turning my troubles over to You.

FIT FOR LIFE

GOD COMES TO TRANSFORM OUR ENTIRE LIVES—MIND, BODY, AND SOUL.

Life expectancy would grow by leaps and bounds if green vegetables smelled as good as bacon.

DOUG LARSON

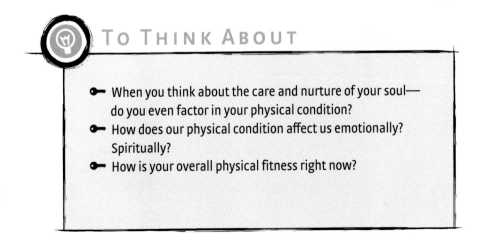

TO THINK ABOUT

- When you think about the care and nurture of your soul— do you even factor in your physical condition?
- How does our physical condition affect us emotionally? Spiritually?
- How is your overall physical fitness right now?

LESSON FOR LIFE

Promises

God will:

Delight in the way He made you
Psalm 139:14-16

Transform your earthly body
Philippians 3:21

Give you strength to bear fruit
2 Peter 1:5-8

Give you His love and patience
2 Thessalonians 3:5

Health of the Body, Health of the Soul

BIBLE STUDY PASSAGE: 1 CORINTHIANS 9:24-27

Because you were bought by God for a price. So honor God with your bodies.

1 CORINTHIANS 6:20

Read the bestsellers list for books any day, any week, any year, and you will always find multiple health, fitness, and diet books there. Cosmetics and beauty aids have always been a huge and profitable industry, but now much more invasive cosmetic surgery treatments are growing and multiplying yearly.

When considering physical fitness as one way to care for your soul, we are not subjecting you to a new assault of unreal and unhealthy expectations of beauty and fitness. Paul's simple admonition is: "Training your body helps you in some ways, but serving God helps you in every way by bringing you blessings in this life and in the future life, too" (1 Timothy 4:8). That suggests that all of us receive benefit from the physical care of our bodies. Benefits of good physical health include—

- *More strength and energy to invest in relationships.*
- *Increased self-control, which is an important part of our Christian walk.*
- *Sharper mental acumen due to the release of endorphins in your brain.*
- *Better emotional health.*
- *Increased self-esteem, which is fed through accomplishing goals.*

But I'm so busy already, I don't have time to exercise. Add thirty minutes to an hour of exercise to your life three or four times a week and discover you have more time.

But I don't have the energy to exercise. *I'm tired.* You might be tired by lack of exercise. Physical energy is not a finite quantity, but a renewable resource. Exercise renews it.

But I've tried to lose weight before and it didn't work. This soul matter isn't about losing weight. It's about improving fitness. Don't worry about your weight.

But how will this help me grow closer to God? Nothing is more important than your relationship with God. Why not listen to Christian music and pray as you walk, run, lift, stretch, bike, or jump rope?

May your soul grow as you start today to take care of your body and mind!

Because you have these blessings, do your best to add these things to your lives: to your faith, add goodness; and to your goodness, add knowledge; and to your knowledge, add self-control; and to your self-control, add patience; and to your patience, add service for God ...

2 Peter 1:5-6

Which Weigh Did She Go?

CANDY ARRINGTON

Although I promised it would never happen, I was overweight and out of shape. Those extra fifteen or twenty pounds that hung on following my pregnancies were still there and multiplying. And although I'd strategized ways to tip the scales in the opposite direction, most of my plotting proved unsuccessful.

As I stood before the mirror, taking body inventory, I knew the time for discipline had arrived. All I really wanted to do was sit down and break my fast with a luscious carbohydrate-laden cinnamon raisin bagel slathered with full-fat cream cheese, but I knew old habits had to change.

I dug through a stack of papers for the health club brochure, half hoping I'd discarded it while finishing off the holiday candy. But there it was—muscular, lean bodies posing under the bold title BODY CHALLENGE. I was tempted to allow the glossy folder to slide unheeded into the trashcan at my feet. Instead, I opened it.

After finding a pair of sweat pants that didn't make me look like a stuffed sausage, I made my way to the gym. The scariest part of the whole regime was not the weight lifting but having BEFORE pictures taken and body fat content assessed. All of this was totally demoralizing, but I reminded myself I was responsible for my current shape.

It took several weeks to learn balancing protein and carb and skinning my fat consumption down to practically nothing, but I was determined. Surprisingly, I was not constantly starving as I'd predicted. Eating several small meals helped.

The workout program was another story. I felt like a total klutz, and why was the gym ringed with mirrors? While all the lean-bodied ones strutted their stuff, I dragged my tiny weights to a corner, lifting with my back to the glass. Three days of weight lifting coupled with three days of cardio exercise became my weekly routine.

At the end of the twelve-week challenge, I was somewhat discouraged that I had lost a mere six pounds. Loss in inches was more significant, so I decided to continue the program on my own. During the summer, I stepped my walking up to running and watched the scales dip into a tens bracket that I hadn't witnessed in years.

While I still struggle with the lure of old habits, I find that praying for discipline every day and confessing moments of eating cheating empowers me to stick to the program.

Early in the endeavor, I begged God for a few pounds off the scales. Now I praise Him for a healthier body, a changed lifestyle, and better eating habits. My meager sacrifices seem small compared to the price Christ paid. The least I can do is honor him with my body.

ACTION STEP

KEEP THIS LESSON SIMPLE. WRITE DOWN AND ACT ON ONE THING YOU CAN DO TODAY IN EACH OF THE FOLLOWING AREAS:

- DIET
- EXERCISE
- MENTAL HEALTH

PRAYER

THANK YOU FOR SENDING YOUR HOLY SPIRIT TO LIVE WITHIN ME. HELP ME HONOR YOUR PRESENCE WITH MY WORDS, THOUGHTS, AND DEEDS.

FAMILY PROBLEMS

WHEN THERE IS STRIFE AND DISAPPOINTMENT WITH THOSE CLOSEST TO US, WE NEED TO RECEIVE AND OFFER EXTRA GRACE AND FORGIVENESS.

God invented parenthood. He is for us. He is for each of our children. He is champion of their lives, their years, their health, their calling, and their eternal destiny.

RALPH T. MATTSON AND THOM BLACK

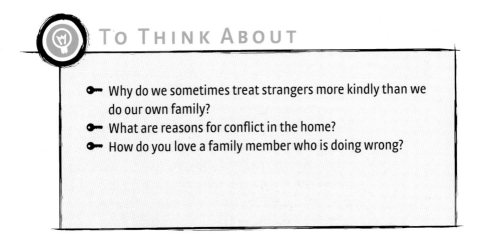

To Think About

- Why do we sometimes treat strangers more kindly than we do our own family?
- What are reasons for conflict in the home?
- How do you love a family member who is doing wrong?

LESSON FOR LIFE

Promises

God will:

Bless your parenting
efforts
Proverbs 22:6

Be your Father
Psalm 68:5
Romans 8:15-16

Offer forgiveness
Isaiah 1:18

Patiently await a
rebellious child
Luke 15:20

Family Feud

BIBLE STUDY PASSAGE: GENESIS 37

God has chosen you and made you his holy people. He loves you. So always do these things: Show mercy to others, be kind, humble, gentle, and patient. Get along with each other, and forgive each other. If someone does wrong to you, forgive that person because the Lord forgave you.

COLOSSIANS 3:12-13

If you are experiencing conflict in your home, don't despair—you are part of a long and proud lineage of family feuds.

Jacob, one of the great fathers of our faith from the Old Testament, had twelve sons. As was the custom of the day, the sons were born of two mothers. Not surprisingly, there was sibling rivalry based on which mother the son was born to, but even more because Jacob clearly favored one of his wives—and especially one of his sons, Joseph. He was resented for his coat of many colors—a singular gift from his dad. He was hated for his dreams, including the one he told to his brothers, predicting that they—and his parents—would bow before him. Not even doting Jacob was crazy about that one.

When the conflict boiled over, Joseph's ten older brothers sold him into slavery and told their father Joseph was dead. While in Egypt, Joseph worked his way up to head of a household, was falsely accused and sent to prison, was forgotten in a dungeon of despair for seven years, and finally ended up as the Pharaoh's most powerful and trusted advisor. Oh, and he also forgave his brothers and saved his own people and that entire region of the world from a great famine.

Not every family meltdown has a storybook ending—it seems impossible when we are in the midst of a crisis. Children rebel and make terrible, self-defeating choices. Sibling rivalry hits epic proportions and turns a home into a battleground. Spouses lose touch. Busy schedules outweigh family bonds.

In Colossians 3:12, Paul says: "Show mercy to others, be kind, humble, gentle, and patient." Maybe you are experiencing conflicts and problems that go beyond civility and preventative medicine right now. Draw comfort from Paul's instructions to "not worry about anything, but pray and ask God for everything you need, always giving thanks. And God's peace, which is so great we cannot understand it, will keep your hearts and minds in Christ Jesus" (Philippians 4:6-7).

And whether in good times or moments of crisis, our greatest step of faith will be to entrust our children to God.

It is good and pleasant when God's people live together in peace!
Psalm 133:1

115

REAL LIFE

My Son, the Prodigal

NANETTE THORSEN-SNIPES

The feeling of terror steals into my life. I watch shards of light dancing in my cup as my husband and I wait for my son to come home. Long ago, my son gave me the mug with brightly painted daisies for my birthday. I cup it in my hands remembering the event. He was always bringing me flowers.

When he became a teen, his anger seemed to erupt over the least thing: One day, he slammed his ten-speed again and again into the red Georgia clay, until it finally lay broken in a heap. I cringed listening to his foul language.

The anger was familiar. His father exhibited the same anger when he threatened me with a loaded gun, prompting me to leave with my two young boys.

One day, Donnie stole a gun from our house. He left that same afternoon and, though we knew of the theft, we had no idea where he was. We just hoped he was safe.

By late that evening, we still hadn't heard from my son. I sat in my recliner, reading my Bible. "I leave you peace; my peace I give you. I do not give it to you as the world does. So don't let your hearts be troubled or afraid" (John 14:27).

In that moment, I felt peace wash over me as I released my son to the Lord. My husband paced the floor a while longer, then headed to bed.

At 2 A.M. the ringing phone awakened us. I answered and learned that Donnie was in jail after fighting with a bouncer at a local hotel. When Security learned he had a gun, they called the police. Donnie ended up in jail.

My husband said with resignation, "I've been praying about this, and I don't think we should get him out again." I knew he was right, but Donnie was my own flesh and blood, and it was hard to turn away. Yet my husband and I remained united.

A few days later, Donnie came home, packed his belongings, and moved out. I didn't hear from him for awhile.

One day, he came to the house with a young woman. We invited them in, and he announced they were getting married. I was delighted to learn of their plans, but was apprehensive about his anger. I prayed, though, that he and his future wife would be happy.

As the months raced by, I saw a change in Donnie. The angry young man melted away and in his place was a young man who had given his life to God.

On one of our first Christmases together after his marriage, Donnie drove to the store with my husband. "Can you ever forgive me for the pain I put you through?" he asked.

My husband smiled and put his arm around him. "I've already forgiven you."

ACTION STEP

HOW MUCH QUALITY TIME DO YOU SPEND AS A FAMILY? ONE LOST TRADITION IS THE IDEA OF A WEEKLY "FAMILY NIGHT." NO ACTIVITIES, NO TV, NO FRIENDS OVER—JUST A TIME FOR GAMES AND DISCUSSION. IF THIS SOUNDS LIKE MORE THAN YOU CAN "FORCE ON" YOUR FAMILY AT THIS TIME, TAKE BABY STEPS, AND FIND SOME WAY TO GET EVERYONE IN THE SAME ROOM ON A REGULAR BASIS.

PRAYER

Father, I place my family into Your loving arms of grace and kindness. As the loving father of Scripture patiently awaited his prodigal son, so I will ever love my children, even if they make bad choices.

GRIEF

PAIN AND SORROW ARE INEVITABLE ASPECTS OF LIFE, BUT GOD IS KIND AND GENTLE AS HE HEALS A BROKEN HEART.

God is closest to those with broken hearts.

JEWISH SAYING

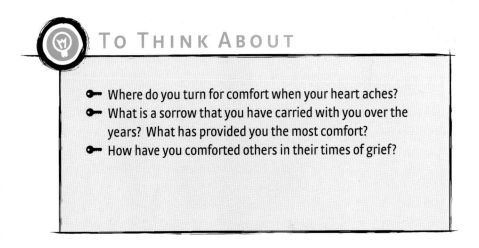

TO THINK ABOUT

- Where do you turn for comfort when your heart aches?
- What is a sorrow that you have carried with you over the years? What has provided you the most comfort?
- How have you comforted others in their times of grief?

LESSON FOR LIFE

Promises

God will:

Put an end to suffering
Revelation 21:4

Heal the grieving
Psalm 147:3

Comfort you
Psalm 94:19

Use you to comfort
others
2 Corinthians 1:4

Comforted Comforters

BIBLE STUDY PASSAGE: 2 CORINTHIANS 1:2-7

He heals the brokenhearted and bandages their wounds.

PSALM 147:3

Grief is assuredly a part of life. Death. Pain. Loss. Separation. If we care about and love someone or something in a way that creates joy, then that same care and love for the person can be turned to sorrow in the face of loss.

Though we can talk about certain stages of grief—denial, anger, bargaining, depression, acceptance (first presented by Elizabeth Kubler-Ross in the book *On Death and Dying*)—there is no set timetable or "cure" for grief. The stages can occur in any variety of sequence, and certain stages may recur and dominate what we are feeling.

The good news is that the God of "all comfort" meets us right where we are. He doesn't ignore our tears, grow impatient with our questions, or condemn us for feelings of anger. He doesn't demand that we "get over it and move on" at some proscribed time. But He does embrace us and cry with us and nurse us back to health and wholeness. God knows the hurt of rejection and the horror of losing His only begotten Son on a cruel cross.

And the comfort He gives to us enables us to comfort others (2 Corinthians 1:4). It doesn't mean we are suddenly wiser and have more words to share—sometimes all a person who is grieving wants is your presence and a shoulder to cry on.

We may never understand why suffering occurs, but we can receive the tender love and compassion of God. And we can hold to the promise of a heavenly home where there are no more tears and sorrow (Revelation 21:4).

When he came near the town gate, he saw a funeral. A mother, who was a widow, had lost her only son. A large crowd from the town was with the mother while her son was being carried out. When the Lord saw her, he felt very sorry for her and said, "Don't cry."
Luke 7:12-13

From Mourning to Morning

LOUISE TUCKER JONES

It had been several sad and lonely weeks since my three-month-old son, Travis, had died suddenly with congenital heart disease. In fact, the weeks had now turned into months, and whereas I held onto God with all my strength right after his death, I now wanted nothing to do with Him. I was so angry at God for taking my son that I vowed to never pray to Him again.

There was just one problem: my four-year-old son, Aaron. He missed his brother dearly and every day he would ask me questions like, "Mommy, what's Heaven like?" "Mommy, can I go to Heaven and see Travis?" Or, "Mommy, why can't Daddy go get Travis and bring him home?" These are tough questions, especially when you are mad at God.

I couldn't stand the thought of hurting Aaron with the bitterness that was consuming me. I had taught him every day of his young life that Jesus loved him. I could not bear to destroy that faith. I knew I had to find peace beyond my grief so that I could be a good mother to Aaron.

Finally, one night, as I lay alone on my bed in the darkened room, I poured out my heart to God—my anger, bitterness, and pain. I prayed, *Lord, I have tried to change, but I can't; so if You want me whole again, You will have to do it.*

Suddenly, the room was filled with an almost palpable peace and I heard God speak to my heart, *Louise, Travis is with Me.* Then, to my amazement, I felt the weight of my baby son placed against by breast and could almost feel his hair brush against my cheek. I couldn't open my eyes as tears streamed across my temples, soaking my hair. I lay absolutely still, allowing God to comfort me in a way I had never known as I continued listening to His gentle whisper, *Travis is okay. He's with Me.*

When I awoke the next morning, the bitterness and anger were gone. I still missed my son terribly. I still had no explanation for the deep why in my heart. But I had the most intimate encounter with God's love and presence than I had ever experienced in my entire life.

ACTION STEP

WHEN SOMEONE FACES THE GRIEF OF A TRAUMATIC LOSS IN THEIR LIFE, THEY OFTEN AREN'T READY TO TALK IMMEDIATELY. THEY SIMPLY NEED A FRIEND TO BE CLOSE. IS THERE SOMEONE FROM YOUR CHURCH, NEIGHBORHOOD, OR COMMUNITY WHO IS IN DEEP GRIEF RIGHT NOW? WHAT SMALL TOKEN OF SUPPORT CAN YOU EXTEND—A MEAL, A SMALL GIFT BOOK, A LETTER? ACT AS SOON AS POSSIBLE.

PRAYER

THANK YOU FOR THE GIFT OF JESUS CHRIST, WHO SUFFERED AND DIED FOR MY SINS, AND WHO UNDERSTANDS ANY SUFFERING I MIGHT EXPERIENCE.

SELF-ACCEPTANCE

THE TRUE AND LASTING MEASURE OF A PERSON'S WORTH AND BEAUTY IS A MATTER OF THE HEART.

No one can make you feel inferior without your consent.

ELEANOR ROOSEVELT

TO THINK ABOUT

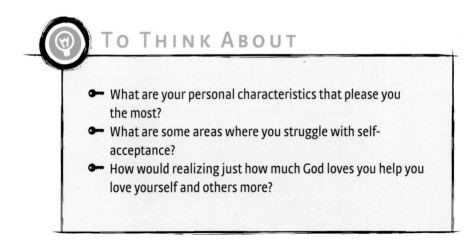

- What are your personal characteristics that please you the most?
- What are some areas where you struggle with self-acceptance?
- How would realizing just how much God loves you help you love yourself and others more?

LESSON FOR LIFE

Promises

God will:

Justify you by your
faith, not your level
of perfection
Galatians 2:16

Honor your inner beauty
Proverbs 15:26
Proverbs 31:30
Psalm 45:11

Delight in you
Psalm 147:10-11

Give you lasting beauty
1 Peter 3:4

Precious in His Sight

BIBLE STUDY PASSAGE: EPHESIANS 3:14-21

In Christ we are set free by the blood of his death, and so we have forgiveness of sins. How rich is God's grace, which he has given to us so fully and freely.

EPHESIANS 1:7-8

Why do we find it so hard to share our true self with others?

One of the great fears of the human race is that if someone were to truly know us—really get to know us at the core of our being—then there is no possible way that they could love and respect us.

The amazing truth of our Bible study verses is that God, who knows us best, also loves us the very most. The verbs found in Ephesians 1 wonderfully describe God's love for us and are powerful expressions of the intensity of His feelings for us: He chooses us; He lavishes grace on us; He predestines us— even before we were born—to be His children. We also read in this chapter that He redeems us and forgives our sins through the sacrifice of Jesus Christ.

What makes this love even more remarkable is that God

doesn't meet our needs in a begrudging manner—*I created them, I guess I have to save them*—but "according to His good pleasure" (v. 9 NKJV). It pleases God to love us. Just as a parent glories in her child, so God glories in us (v. 12).

But how well does God really know me? Does He really understand how bad and ugly my attitudes and actions have been? Be assured, God knows everything—and He lavishes His love on you with full wisdom and understanding (v. 8).

If the two great needs of being human are to love and to be loved, then you are doubly blessed because of God's love for you. That gives you all the reasons and resources you need to love others—and yourself.

But God shows his great love for us in this way: Christ died for us while we were still sinners.
Romans 5:8

REAL LIFE

I'm Getting Older and Better

JOAN CLAYTON

"Aren't you the Mrs. Clayton who used to teach first grade?" I didn't remember the woman's face, but I politely replied, "Yes."

"Well, I didn't recognize you at first, but that was a long time ago—and time sure doesn't stand still."

Now I had two choices. That statement could ruin my day or I could keep my joy. I tried to do laugh it off and smooth things over with the lady, but I was having trouble continuing the conversation. So to keep my cool, I walked away with a "see ya."

I tried to push the comments out of my mind. Each time I thought about it, rejection tried to rule the day.

When I told my husband about the incident, he hugged me tight. "To me, you're the most beautiful woman in the world."

When I read my daily Bible reading that night, it just so happened I read Psalm 45. I came to verse 11: "So shall the king greatly desire thy beauty: for he is thy Lord; and worship thou him."

Lord, you think I'm beautiful.

I read verse 13: "The king's daughter is all glorious within: her clothing is of wrought gold."

Lord, you think I'm glorious within.

I read verse 17: "I will make thy name to be remembered in all generations: therefore shall the people praise thee for ever and ever."

Lord, you will make my name remembered to all my descendants.

What else could I ever want? The Lord thinks I'm beautiful, so what do I care if someone thinks I've aged? The Lord loves me just like I am.

Right then, I shouted, "Thank You, Lord!"

No one stays young looking forever. Everyone ages. And each stage of life has its own unique beauty. God sees the heart, and that makes all the difference.

I have seen a person's self-esteem go down the tube as they begin to get older. Not only do they feel tacky in appearance, but feel useless and unwanted. Our culture puts a premium on youth and beauty. TV is flooded with products that supposedly keep us young looking. The underlying message is we are not okay the way we are. That is the biggest lie the enemy ever dreamed up.

The Lord's plan for me doesn't end with the advancement of age. Besides, some of the greatest contributors to society were in their older years.

The next time someone tells me I have aged, I will say, "Yes, but you should see me on the inside. My spirit is becoming younger and more beautiful by the minute." I "stay fresh and green and bring forth fruit in old age" (Psalm 92:14). I am being changed from one degree of glory to another.

Because of Jesus, I have the hidden beauty of the heart and that makes me older and better.

The Lord and my husband—they both think I'm beautiful!

ACTION STEP

TAKE A RELAXED THIRTY-MINUTE WALK BY YOURSELF, SPENDING THE ENTIRE TIME THANKING GOD THAT HE LOVES YOU SO MUCH AND SEES TREMENDOUS BEAUTY WITHIN EVERY SINGLE AREA YOUR LIFE. WHEN YOU GET BACK HOME, CAN YOU COUNT HOW MANY WAYS GOD FINDS YOU TO BE BEAUTIFUL?

PRAYER

As my Creator, You knew me before I was even born. You know everything about me—my strengths, weaknesses, and idiosyncrasies. Thank You for loving me as I am. Thank You for making me beautiful from the inside out.

FATIGUE

WEARINESS TAKES ITS TOLL ON BOTH BODY AND SOUL, SO THE WISE WOMAN COMPLEMENTS WORK WITH REST, PLAY, AND WORSHIP IN HER LIFE.

Any mother could perform the jobs of several air traffic controllers with ease.

LISA ALTHER

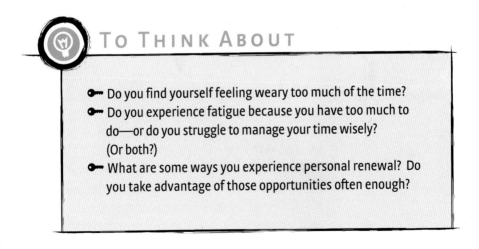

TO THINK ABOUT

- ☞ Do you find yourself feeling weary too much of the time?
- ☞ Do you experience fatigue because you have too much to do—or do you struggle to manage your time wisely? (Or both?)
- ☞ What are some ways you experience personal renewal? Do you take advantage of those opportunities often enough?

LESSON FOR LIFE

Promises

God will:

Produce in you
perseverance
Romans 5:3

Perfect your character
James 1:2-4

Strengthen you
Philippians 4:13

Give you endurance
and joy
Colossians 1:11-12

Rest for the Weary

BIBLE STUDY PASSAGE: PSALM 73:23-28

He gives strength to those who are tired and more power to those who are weak. Even children become tired and need to rest, and young people trip and fall. But the people who trust the Lord will become strong again. They will rise up as an eagle in the sky; they will run and not need rest; they will walk and not become tired.

ISAIAH 40:29-31

If you ever struggle with the discouragement that comes from fatigue, you are in good company—

- *Moses, one of the greatest leaders in the history of humankind, became so exasperated from the grumblings of the Israelites that he lashed out in anger, bringing God's judgment on him (see Numbers 20:2-13).*
- *The prophet Elijah was so tired from standing alone for God against false prophets that he withdrew from the world and said that he preferred death over life (see 1 Kings 19:3-9)!*
- *David, while waiting to assume the throne promised to him by*

God, felt so beset by his enemies that he wrote numerous Psalms of lament and sorrow (see Psalms 59, 69, and 72).
- *Even Jesus, Son of God (but fully man), was so discouraged and weary in the Garden of Gethsemane, that He longed to have His friends beside Him in this moment of acute need (see Mark 14:32-42).*

None of us are immune from the effects of fatigue on our body, mind, and spirit. No wonder it is so important that we continually seek and create ways to balance work, rest, play, and worship if we are to be at our very best.

In addition to using our time and resources more wisely, we must turn to the Giver of life, God himself, who will bring renewal to even the weariest spirit. All that's required is trust: trust that God loves you and will minister to your spirit. That's what God did for Moses, David, Elijah, and other heroes of faith—and that's what He will do for you.

But now we groan in this tent. We want God to give us our heavenly home.
2 Corinthians 5:2

REAL LIFE

Harvest of Strength

LISA ERLER

I wanted a nap. My eyes felt droopy all morning, and I yawned all through lunch. Elisabeth needed her bottle. Rachael wanted to watch Snow White with me in my bedroom. Lying on my bed and dozing, I fed the baby and watched the movie in snips. Blink. "Mirror, Mirror, on the Wall." Blink. Snow White running through the forest. Blink.

My Shih Tzu jumped on my legs, and my eyes popped open.

I carried Elisabeth to her crib. One more gaze at her perfect heart-shaped mouth and the fan of golden lashes resting on her cheek, and I left her to sleep.

On my way back to bed, Matthew, my home-schooled fifth grader, called me, needing help with his Bible lesson. We read the book of Ruth. "What's gleaning?" Matthew asked when we read the part about Ruth picking up the leftover grain behind the harvesters. I yawned and explained it to my son, thinking nothing of it. I was too swept up in the romance of the story. I could picture Ruth as she lay at Boaz's feet. I could see him reaching his hand out for hers at their wedding.

"So you see, Matthew, Ruth was the great grandmother of David, and you remember who he was, right?"

"Yeah, he was the guy who flung the stone into the giant's head. Hey, Mom! Why did they like to keep the head of an enemy? It only sat there and rotted.

What's the point?"

I shook my head at the colorful world of boys and said, "I don't know, but I'm taking a nap, Matthew. Answer the questions now, and remember neat handwriting and spell words correctly."

I dozed through the rest of Snow White, and afterwards, I scratched Rachael's back until she fell asleep. Just as I was drifting off, Elisabeth woke up. I didn't know whether to laugh or cry. I knew I wasn't going to get a nap this particular day.

Later, I found a moment to write in my journal. "Lord, I'm tired! I didn't get a nap. I have laundry in baskets to fold, and James is going to be home from school any minute. Help! Where is my rest? I just can't do this job anymore."

I sat for a moment in sulky silence and watched the baby's glee in jumping up and down in her seat. For a moment, even her happiness could not break through the haze of my fatigue. But then I did laugh. And cried. And prayed. And thanked God for beautiful children, the opportunity to stay at home and care for them, and for knowing exactly what I need to smile in my heart again.

Through the kindness and mercy of God and others, Naomi gathered the wheat she and Ruth needed for sustenance. Through the kindness and mercy of God and a bouncing baby, I gathered the strength I need to face my day.

ACTION STEP

VISIT A LOCAL BOOKSTORE OR LIBRARY AND SELECT A BOOK ON TIME MANAGE-
MENT—OR DO A SIMPLE INTERNET SEARCH AND READ SOME FREE ARTICLES
ON KEEPING LIFE IN BALANCE. YOUR GOAL IS TO FIND ONE PRINCIPLE YOU
CAN PUT INTO PRACTICE THAT VERY DAY! MOST IMPORTANTLY, PLAN TO GO TO
BED "ON TIME" EVERY NIGHT THIS WEEK!

PRAYER

*Heavenly Father, I come to You with a weary spirit, asking You to renew my
strength. Give me the wisdom to take care of myself.*

MARRIAGE

THE LOVE AND HONOR YOU SHOW YOUR HUSBAND SPILLS OVER AND BLESSES YOU AND OTHERS IN ALL AREAS OF YOUR LIFE.

One advantage of marriage is that, when you fall out of love with him or he falls out of love with you, it keeps you together until you fall in again.

JUDITH VIORST

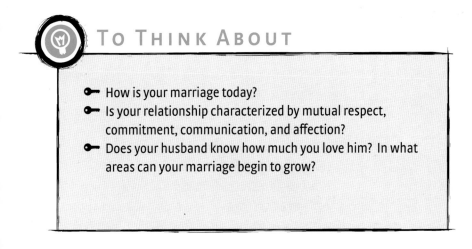

To Think About

- How is your marriage today?
- Is your relationship characterized by mutual respect, commitment, communication, and affection?
- Does your husband know how much you love him? In what areas can your marriage begin to grow?

LESSON FOR LIFE

Promises

God will:

Bless your relationships
as you adopt a forgiving
attitude
Proverbs 17:9

Be pleased as you keep
peace
Psalm 133:1

Perfect all virtues as you
cultivate love
Colossians 3:14

Honor One Another

BIBLE STUDY PASSAGE: EPHESIANS 5:21-33

Yield to obey each other because you respect Christ.

EPHESIANS 5:21

One of the most hotly debated Bible verses in modern history is where Paul instructs wives to "submit to your husbands as to the Lord" (Ephesians 5:22 NKJV). However, all you have to do is look back one verse and any argument that Paul was unfair to women and must somehow be reinterpreted becomes moot. There Paul instructs husbands and wives to "submit to one another." Later in the chapter, Paul commands husbands to love their wives as Christ loved the church, which means they must be ready to pay the ultimate sacrifice (Ephesians 5:25). In the traditional wedding vows, both husband and wife promise to the other that they will love, honor, comfort, keep in sickness and health, forsake all others, and be true as long as both are alive.

Despite such clear, simple biblical admonitions and marital vows, too many marriages are not characterized by love, honor, comfort, keeping, and forsaking. In too many marriages, not nearly enough mutual submission takes place. Paul says: "Let each of you look out not only for his own interests, but also for the interests of others" (Philippians 2:4 NKJV). It's fair to say that the source of most marital strife is when one or the other spouse is primarily looking out for his or her interests.

The key to building your marriage and loving your husband, then, is very simple—but can be oh so hard. You must look first to his interests.

Wait a minute. That's not fair. And what if he doesn't reciprocate?

Fairness and reciprocity are important. But true love is not always fair and not always returned in kind. And what God wants you to do is to love and honor your husband—and trust your husband's response into His hands.

Does that mean I have to be a doormat?

God does not want you to cast aside your personality, thoughts, perspectives, and life. Remember, His ideal is mutuality. So He does want you—just as He wants your husband—to be the first to love, honor, forgive, and be faithful if that's what is required. In the mysterious ways that God works and changes lives, nothing will bless you, your children, your friends, and yes, your husband, more than a spirit of love.

Love is patient and kind. Love is not jealous, it does not brag, and it is not proud. Love is not rude, is not selfish, and does not get upset with others. Love does not count up wrongs that have been done. Love is not happy with evil but is happy with the truth. Love patiently accepts all things. It always trusts, always hopes, and always remains strong.
1 Corinthians 13:4-7

REAL LIFE

A Marriage Made in Heaven

KAREN R. KILBY

We sat across the kitchen table from each other, not quite knowing what to say. We had just come from a counseling session with our pastor. It was my hope that if anyone had the answer to saving our marriage, it would be God. The pastor's advice was what I expected: If we trusted God to be a part of our marriage, He would help us overcome our differences.

"Well," David said to me when we got home, "you're the one with the connection to God." Then he got up and left for work. Ouch.

How good it felt to be connected to God—but I wanted to be connected to David too. We had been married for ten years and had four beautiful children and a lovely home. Anyone looking at us from the outside would have thought we had it all together. The truth was we were on the verge of a separation.

As I contemplated what David had said, the thought came that I should call him and say, "I love you." Where in the world did that come from? God must certainly know I didn't feel that. But the thought persisted—it was as if God was telling me He would give me what I needed when I needed it. David's response was, "You don't know how much I needed to hear that." When I hung up, I thought, *Great!* Then it hit me. David would be home at 5:00—then what? God suggested I meet him at the door with a hug and kiss, assuring me again that He would give me what I needed when I needed it. And He did! I realized another test was coming up when it was bedtime. *Oh, Lord, what now?* I prayed. God's gentle prompt was, "Remember that little red nightie in the bottom drawer?" I argued, *But I can't fake this!* God said, "Obey Me and I will give you what you need when you need it." Did He ever!

I began to understand that it wasn't what David could do for me—it was what I could do for him. What a different way of living and loving than what I was capable of on my own. I began to choose God's unconditional love for David over my natural instinct to be unforgiving and selfish.

David saw the changes in me and began to respond to God's love himself. The Bible says, "When someone becomes a Christian, he becomes a brand new person inside. He's not the same anymore. A new life has begun." That's what happened to us.

Over the years, the strength of our love and faith in God has enabled us to face many difficulties: teenage rebellion, a family member battling substance abuse, losing a friend to suicide, financial problems, even David's heart attack. In all situations, we have found God to be trustworthy, and we know that our security is in His hands—not just today but for all of our tomorrows.

ACTION STEP

WRITE DOWN SEVEN WAYS YOU CAN SHOW RESPECT AND LOVE TO YOUR HUSBAND—BOTH THINGS YOU ARE DOING NOW THAT ARE APPRECIATED, AND NEW WAYS YOU CAN AFFIRM HIM. PRACTICE AT LEAST ONE EACH DAY OVER THE NEXT WEEK. AT THE END OF THE SEVEN DAYS, REFLECT ON WAYS HE RESPONDED TO YOUR STEPS OF FAITH.

PRAYER

Dear Heavenly Father, thank You for my husband and my marriage. I commit myself to You—and to him. Help me to share with him the love You have put in my heart.

SELF-IMPROVEMENT

GOD BLESSES US WITH TALENTS AND GIFTS THAT WE ARE TO DEVELOP AND SHARE WITH OTHERS.

Don't start living tomorrow, tomorrow never arrives.
Start working on your dreams and ambitions today.

UNKNOWN AUTHOR

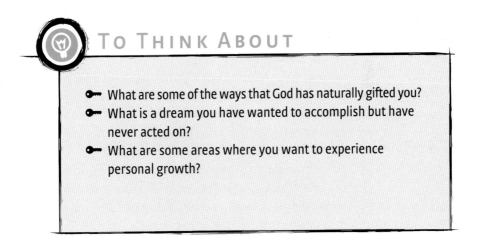

TO THINK ABOUT

- What are some of the ways that God has naturally gifted you?
- What is a dream you have wanted to accomplish but have never acted on?
- What are some areas where you want to experience personal growth?

LESSON FOR LIFE

Promises

God will:

Cause you to flourish
Isaiah 58:11

Bear fruit in your life
John 15:4-5

Give you more as you
are fruitful with what
you have
Matthew 25:21

To Whom Much Is Given

BIBLE STUDY PASSAGE: MATTHEW 25:14-30

God began doing a good work in you, and I am sure he will continue it until it is finished when Jesus Christ comes again.

PHILIPPIANS 1:6

What's wrong with accepting myself as I am? Why do we put so much emphasis on being better and "the best" in our society? Is that any way to live?

No question, we can love ourselves for who we are because God does. And no, we don't have to join a "rat race" of competing with others to have the nicest house and most possessions. We need not push our kids into every activity to ensure that they are smartest and most athletic. No, we cannot prove to God that we are worthy of salvation. Yes, we can relax and savor what we have and enjoy who we are.

But we must also be mindful that "from everyone who has been given much, much will be demanded" (Luke 12:48). In speaking of our salvation, Paul says: "You did not save yourselves; it was a gift from God. It was not the result of your own efforts, so you cannot brag about it. God has made us what we are. In Christ Jesus, God made us to do good works, which God planned in advance for us to live our lives doing" (Ephesians 2:8-10). Notice that God has prepared works for each of us to accomplish. He has given each of us talents and gifts that we are to expand and invest into others: Paul compares the church to a body, each part having a different function that ultimately serves the whole (See Romans 12:5-8).

Consider a couple of challenges and reminders in the area of self-improvement—

The master answered, "You did well. You are a good and loyal servant. Because you were loyal with small things, I will let you care for much greater things. Come and share my joy with me."
Matthew 25:21

- *We don't tend to stay in the same spot—we either move forward or backward.*
- *Big dreams and tasks begin with small steps—what can you do today?*
- *We aren't supposed to be someone else—grow with the dreams and aspirations God has placed in your own heart.*
- *Work is part of the cycle of life—which also includes rest, play, and worship.*
- *Wanting to grow is not selfish—it is the way God created us.*
- *We grow to make ourselves better—and to better serve God.*
- *Discipline is a tremendous source of freedom—from doubt, fear, and lethargy.*

REAL LIFE

Back to School

JENNIFER JOHNSON

"What's wrong with now, Jen? Do you really want to wait till your youngest graduates to start college?"

I gawked at my friend Robin. Sure, she'd held a part-time job, juggled the responsibilities of a husband and two boys, and taken two college classes for the last several months, but I believed her to be a bit demented, or at the very least the owner of a few loose screws.

Yes, I wanted to go to college. I'd dreamed of it for more years than I could recall. Listening to her talk about homework and test dates gave me frequent attacks from that awful green monster. Okay, I must be the one loony. Who in their right mind would feel envy toward someone who had to stay up well past midnight to study for a test?

Me. That's who felt jealous. Me.

I wanted to go back to school. I longed to be in classes with Robin. I wanted to pull my hair out trying to pack sometimes-useless knowledge into my brain. I wanted to earn my college degree.

But how could I? My husband worked like a dog, but earned modest wages. We needed my part-time job to make ends meet. After all, raising three daughters did not happen cost free. How could I possibly go?

"Why don't you just pray about it, Jen?"

146

Well, there was a novel idea, and not a bad one either. I started to pray. *God, Robin's given me this great, impossible idea. I'd like to go, but I don't see how it's possible. Al probably won't go for it either. What do You think?*

The little wheels in my head began to churn. Suddenly, I remembered our van would be paid off before the fall school session began. Hmm, was that my overactive imagination, or was it a prompting from the Holy Spirit?

I decided to try my hand with my hubby, Al. *God, if You want me to go to college, You'll make Al want me to go to college.*

"Al, what do you think about me going to college?"

"What?"

"Well, we'll have the van paid off by fall, and I've always wanted to go to school, and—"

"Go. I want you to. We'll work it out."

I was stunned. I called my friend and told her I'd be attending the University of Kentucky with her next semester. She was thrilled.

Almost four years have passed since I walked into my first class, English 101. I was the oldest person in the room, including my teacher. Now, I can see the light at the end of the tunnel.

My precious friend graduates in one month. I will graduate the semester after her. God worked it out for me to go. He worked it out to see me through. God cares about the longings of my heart—or maybe He put the longing there in the beginning. He just needed me to be willing to trust—and act.

ACTION STEP

WHAT IS ONE AREA OF YOUR LIFE WHERE YOU WOULD LIKE TO GROW? WRITE OUT THE FOLLOWING STEPS:

1. WHAT IS YOUR GOAL?
2. HOW LONG WILL IT TAKE TO ACHIEVE THAT GOAL?
3. WHAT RESOURCES DO YOU NEED?
4. WHAT ARE HINDRANCES AND DISCOURAGEMENTS YOU WILL FACE?
5. WHAT IS YOUR FIRST STEP?

PRAYER

Thank You for giving me so many talents and opportunities, O Lord. Help me to honor You and bless others as I accomplish the dreams You've planted in my heart.

GOD'S TIMING

GOD IS NOT INTERESTED IN OUR INSTANT GRATIFICATION, BUT IN OUR FULFILLING HIS PLANS AND PURPOSES OVER A LIFETIME.

Remember you are very special to God as His precious child.
He has promised to complete the good work He has begun in you.

GARY SMALLEY AND JOHN TRENT

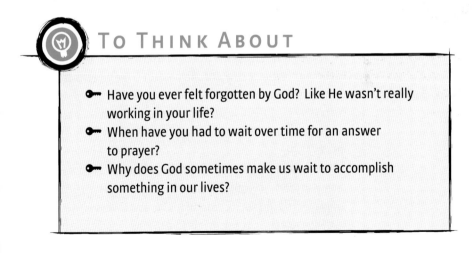

TO THINK ABOUT

- Have you ever felt forgotten by God? Like He wasn't really working in your life?
- When have you had to wait over time for an answer to prayer?
- Why does God sometimes make us wait to accomplish something in our lives?

LESSON FOR LIFE

Promises

God will:

Give wisdom and
provision
Isaiah 28:29

Accomplish His plans
Proverbs 19:21

Always remember you
Nahum 1:7

Give all things for
you to enjoy
1 Timothy 6:17

Hold On

BIBLE STUDY PASSAGE: GENESIS 50:15-26

You meant to hurt me, but God turned your evil into good to save the lives of many people, which is being done.

GENESIS 50:20

God promised to make Abraham the father of a great nation, with descendants as numerous as the stars in the sky (Genesis 15:5). Despite his great faith, can you blame him for questioning when this was going to happen when he was still fatherless at age 75 (Genesis 12:4)?

Samuel anointed David as king of Israel in response to Saul's spirit of disobedience (1 Samuel 16:1). The problem is David was hunted like a fugitive and animal for the next seven years (1 Samuel 19:9). No wonder he cried to God, "Why have you forgotten me? Why am I sad and troubled by my enemies?" (Psalm 42:9).

Moses led the Hebrew slaves from captivity and into the Promised Land—over the course of forty years (Exodus 16:35). Jesus spent the first thirty years of His life as a child, son, student, brother, and carpenter before the right moment came for Him to begin His ministry (Luke 3:23).

Why doesn't God just bring about His plans in our lives right now? Could it be that one of the most important ways God forms us into the image of His Son Jesus Christ is through allowing us to express our faith in Him through waiting?

In the Proverb, Solomon points out the natural truism that "It is sad not to get what you hoped for. But wishes that come true are like eating fruit from the tree of life" (13:12). But Paul's testimony that "The sufferings we have now are nothing compared to the great glory that will be shown to us" (Romans 8:18) is a powerful reminder that God may not be early—but He's always right on time with just what we need.

Is your soul weary with worry? Are you frustrated waiting to know God wants to do in your life? Hold on. God is on the way right now.

Lord, you are my God. I honor you and praise you, because you have done amazing things. You have always done what you said you would do; you have done what you planned long ago.
Isaiah 25:1

REAL LIFE

The Wait

DIANE H. PITTS

At the age of 32, I decided I was through with relationships—it was time to get on with my career, once and for all. Just when I had given up on the idea of marriage, though, God decided it was time to change my mind.

One particular Saturday afternoon, I took a break from my physical therapy studies to look over a list of possible internships. *What a great way to start fresh. I'll intern in some of these places and then move to one of them.* Tennessee, North Carolina, and Pennsylvania sounded like good places to pursue a career and never look back.

I thought back on the past year. I left a secure nursing job for physical therapy school. Although I was working three jobs just to make ends meet, my life wasn't bleak—I had lots of friends, a warm church family, and a promising profession. But the "right" relationship just hadn't materialized. Haven't I waited long enough?

With a stroke of the pen, I filled out my application for internships. *No one would want to go that far away from home,* I reasoned. Nobody but me! My heart ached from disappointment, so I closed it off from further pain. God didn't seem to be doing anything, so why leave Him room to try?

The following morning, I arrived at church as usual, but I went through Sunday school and the morning service on autopilot. I played the piano, but my mind roamed through Amish country and the hills of Pennsylvania. I didn't notice a pair of startling blue eyes watching my every move. After the service, the owner of the eyes questioned a few Sunday morning stragglers.

"Diane? She's single. Been a nurse, but now she's going back to physical therapy school," said a mutual friend.

A young woman interested in Mr. Blue Eyes offered, "The way Diane works and studies, she may not have time to go anywhere."

One more chimed in, "If you're thinking of getting to know her, you better hurry. Yesterday Diane told me she was planning to leave the area after internships."

In the following weeks whenever I was with friends, there was a newcomer—a man with an appealing smile, quick laugh, and piercing blue eyes. Darrell became a constant presence, but not too close. I was so intent on moving away that I missed his strategy. Before I knew it, we were getting to know each other, sharing ideas, and going places. On December 12, less than a month before I left for Memphis, Darrell made it clear that he and God wanted to change my mind about marriage.

In our wedding ceremony a year later, we quoted King Solomon, who said that God has made everything beautiful in its time.

ACTION STEP

SET UP A TIME TO VISIT WITH A SENIOR CITIZEN WHO HAS EXEMPLIFIED A JOYFUL AND FAITHFUL WALK WITH GOD. ASK THE PERSON TO SHARE A FEW STORIES ABOUT WHEN THEY HAD TO WAIT PATIENTLY FOR GOD TO ACT ON A SPECIAL NEED IN HIS OR HER LIFE.

PRAYER

Great is Your faithfulness, O God, my Redeemer. Thank You for being true to Your word by never leaving or forsaking me.

RECEIVING GOD'S MERCY

WHEN WE MAKE A MESS OF LIFE THROUGH DISOBEDIENCE, OUR ONLY HOPE IS THE MERCY OF GOD.

Humanity is never so beautiful as when praying
for forgiveness, or else forgiving one another.

JEAN PAUL RICHTER

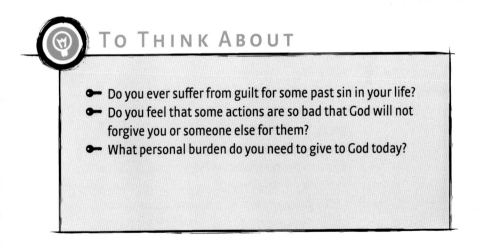

TO THINK ABOUT

- Do you ever suffer from guilt for some past sin in your life?
- Do you feel that some actions are so bad that God will not forgive you or someone else for them?
- What personal burden do you need to give to God today?

LESSON FOR LIFE

Promises

God will:

Be merciful to you
Psalm 103:8

Heal your disobedience
Jeremiah 3:22

Reconcile Himself to you
Colossians 1:22

Forgive you
Jeremiah 50:20

The Beauty of God's Mercy

BIBLE STUDY PASSAGE: PSALM 51

God, be merciful to me because you are loving. Because you are always ready to be merciful, wipe out all my wrongs. Wash away all my guilt and make me clean again.

PSALM 51:1-2

Even the great heroes of the Bible had serious character flaws and were in need of God's mercy.

Jacob, the son of Isaac and one of the fathers of our faith, tricked his twin brother and even his beloved father, in order to "steal" the family birthright (Genesis 25-27).

Moses, who led the Hebrew slaves from the Pharaoh's oppression in Egypt, murdered a man and lived as a fugitive for forty years (Exodus 2-3).

David, perhaps the most beloved and popular of Israel's kings throughout history, performed many acts of courage, faith, and mercy—slaying the giant, Goliath, and sparing King Saul, a sworn enemy to him, to name just two—but also had a litany of sins and shortcomings strewn along his past.

His greatest crime was what he did to Uriah the Hittite, one of his bravest and most loyal soldiers. David coveted and then "took" Uriah's wife, Bathsheba, to be his own. To make his evil act even worse, he had Uriah killed to try and cover up what he had done. (See 2 Samuel 11-12 for the whole story.)

Throughout the Psalms, and especially in Psalm 51, David cries for God's mercy. He knows that being the king doesn't get him off the hook. He knows that no act of contrition can undo his evil deeds.

Only God's mercy can enter a darkened heart and make it pure again.

My guilt has over-whelmed me; like a load it weighs me down.
Psalm 38:4

REAL LIFE

A Heavy Weight

DIANNA GAY

In my mind, I had no choice. What else could I do? Just days from my sixteenth birthday, two pink lines on a white stick spelled my future.

They said the procedure would take two days. I don't recall all the details—only the horrifying ones. The purple pamphlets at the clinic lied. Abortion is not simple. Life does not go on as usual.

With a cup of lukewarm coffee in the bleak waiting room, my entire body ached. My heart felt numb. The repercussions of what just happened sank in. From that moment on, nothing was the same.

A small voice came with me everywhere I went. *How old would I be now if you'd let me live?*

Four years later, I walked into Ed's Trading Post, a tourist trap with coffee mugs and T-shirts. Ed gave me a once-over with squinted eye before hiring me.

One day, he asked me a startling question: "If you died today, where would you go?"

I didn't have a very firm answer. But Ed didn't give up. He talked about Jesus every day. I listened. After all, if he wanted to preach while I was on the clock, why complain?

The next summer, he gave me a Bible. Intrigued that someone would invest in me, I delved in.

My questions came about what I read. Ed answered.

Two years passed. On a dreary Tuesday morning, Ed asked, "If you believe in Jesus and that He died for you, why not invite Him into your life right now?"

He knelt, and I awkwardly followed his lead. He started praying. I don't remember what he said, but I knew I had to say something too.

"God," I began feebly, "I know I haven't talked to You much—"

With those words, my heart ripped open. I sobbed, crying to God for the first time. I didn't deserve Him, or what He did for me.

In that second, a physical weight lifted from my shoulders. The familiar, suffocating weight simply left. I remember my surprise and relief at God's spiritual healing.

This is My burden now. Never worry or be ashamed again.

But even today, twelve years from the day I first heard an unborn child speak to my broken heart, Satan whispers, "Are you sure that was real? Is God even real? How can God forgive you?"

Despite my doubts, I remember. Jesus lifted my unforgivable decision and made it His own. That moment changed me and is eternalized in my heart.

I've heard miracles defined as naturally impossible events. But the salvation of a broken spirit is miraculous, too. Without Jesus, it couldn't happen. My final life decision is to love and serve Him, for He granted the miracle of lifting such a heavy, heavy weight.

ACTION STEP

READ ALL OF PSALM 51. NOW WRITE YOUR OWN "SONG" TO GOD, ASKING HIM TO MAKE YOUR HEART AND LIFE PURE BEFORE HIM AND THE PEOPLE IN YOUR LIFE.

PRAYER

Cleanse me from my past—and deliver me from any temptations in my life right now—as you make me into the beautiful woman You have created me to be, O God.

PERSEVERANCE

MANY OF LIFE'S MOST VALUABLE EXPERIENCES DON'T COME EASY AND REQUIRE A SPIRIT OF PERSEVERANCE.

Perseverance is the hard work you do after you get tired of doing the hard work you already did.

NEWT GINGRICH

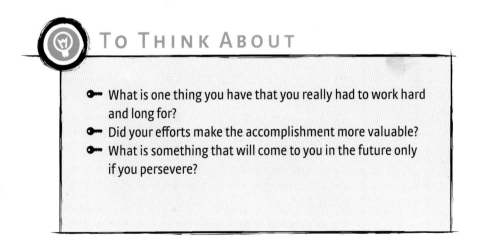

TO THINK ABOUT

- What is one thing you have that you really had to work hard and long for?
- Did your efforts make the accomplishment more valuable?
- What is something that will come to you in the future only if you persevere?

LESSON FOR LIFE

Promises

God will:

Encourage you by His
faithfulness
Hebrews 6:18-19

Produce character in you
Romans 5:4

Bring His plan to comple-
tion in you
1 Peter 1:13

Increase your strength
as you persevere
Job 17:9

Stand Firm

BIBLE STUDY PASSAGE: HEBREWS 12:1-4

We also have joy with our troubles, because we know that these troubles produce patience. And patience produces character, and character produces hope. And this hope will never disappoint us, because God has poured out his love to fill our hearts. He gave us his love through the Holy Spirit, whom God has given to us.

ROMANS 5:3-5

We live in the age of instant gratification. We look at our teenagers and young adults and click our tongues because they want only the best now—new cars, new clothes, new toys, and lots of debt. But they learned those values and attitudes somewhere!

But perhaps even more disconcerting than an impatient, acquisitive spirit is the refusal to pursue good, noble, worthy dreams because they don't come soon, easy, or conveniently enough. Esau traded his family birthright for a bowl of soup because he was hungry now (Genesis 25:29-34). Saul lost his kingship because of greed (1 Samuel 15:7-11) and fear of the future (1 Samuel 28:7, 1 Chronicles 10:13). The rich young ruler sadly chose not to follow Jesus because the cost was too high (Luke 18:22-24).

Did you know that perseverance and failure cannot coexist? Why? Failure only happens when you quit. Whether it be a relationship, a spiritual issue, or a personal soul, as long as you keep trying, you are in the game.

The writer of Hebrews calls for his persecuted flock of Christians to "not get tired and stop trying" (12:3). He reminds them that in tough times, if we want to win the race, we must get rid of things that hinder us and sin that entangles us. We can't run with extra weight and cords around our ankles. But even more importantly, he calls all of us to keep our eyes on Jesus, the author and perfector of our faith, who showed us how to run the race with perseverance. When we see our final destination and know that others have gone before us, it makes even the difficult moments of the journey more than bearable.

Though there are accomplishments and spiritual growth that happen because of a quick spirit, the matters of greatest importance are usually more like a marathon. The good news is that Jesus runs beside us each step of the way.

Ask, and God will give to you. Search, and you will find. Knock, and the door will open for you.

Matthew 7:7

REAL LIFE

If You Don't Climb the Mountain, You Can't Get the View

LINDA RONDEAU

I thrust a tired hand on the flat, rocky surface and with an assist from my husband landed on the top of Lion Mountain. I had prevailed. If this had been a Rocky movie, I might have even jumped up and down with my fists in the air.

Once a year, I force myself to take to the hills and climb one of the peaks near our home in the Adirondack area. Being overweight and asthmatic as well as afraid of heights, climbing a mountain is perhaps one of the hardest things for me to do. While I can walk a straight line for miles, as soon as I start an incline, my lungs object. I'm ready for a shot of Albuterol before I finish the first quarter mile. Like an exasperated two-year-old, I moan, "Are we there yet?"

As difficult as climbing is for me, though, the hardship seems inconsequential when I get to the summit. The surrounding beauty fills me with so much awe I barely remember that I'm in pain. From the top of the mountain, I get a small sense of what God must see when He views the world.

This particular climb was harder. It was fall—a tough season for asthmatics. I hated that my husband had to get behind and nearly push me through the steepest part, just before the top. My daughter, as thin as Scarlett O'Hara, stayed right by me, sometimes offering me a drink of water and letting me rest until my lungs filled back up. Just when I was ready to quit and start back down, sunlight broke through the cloud of trees above me. I was nearly there. The realization filled me with renewed determination. On all fours, I crawled the rest of the way and sighed with relief when I lay prone, exhausted from the day's exertion.

After taking two puffs on my inhaler, I righted myself and nodded to the claps of celebration from family and a few other climbers who politely resisted laughing at my ashen face. As I basked in the circus of colors below, my heart gave praise to the Creator of such wonders. I thanked God for not letting me quit when the way was rough and for the support of loved ones on the journey. I discovered something that day: At the apex of revelation, I should be grateful for the hardship that brought me to the point of sight. For I could not have experienced it any other way.

ACTION STEP

IF LIFE IS MORE LIKE A MARATHON THAN A SPRINT, WHY NOT WALK OR RUN YOUR OWN PERSONAL MARATHON TODAY? NO, YOU DON'T HAVE TO COVER TWENTY-SIX MILES ON FOOT, BUT PLOT OUT A NICE, LONG, ONE-HOUR COURSE, AND SPEND THE TIME TALKING TO GOD ABOUT THE VARIOUS CHALLENGES YOU ARE FACING NOW, THANKING HIM FOR HIS HELP EACH STEP OF YOUR JOURNEY AHEAD, AND PRAISING HIM THAT HE LOVES YOU AND CARES ABOUT ALL AREAS OF YOUR LIFE.

PRAYER

Thank You, Heavenly Father, that no matter what challenges I face today and tomorrow, You provide me with the physical, emotional, and spiritual resources that I need.

IN-LAWS

SOME RELATIONSHIPS ARE EASY AND SOME ARE DIFFICULT, BUT GOD IS ALWAYS ABLE TO USE OTHERS TO HELP US GROW.

When our relationships are born in the heart of God,
they bring out the best in us, for they are nurtured by love.

DON LESSIN

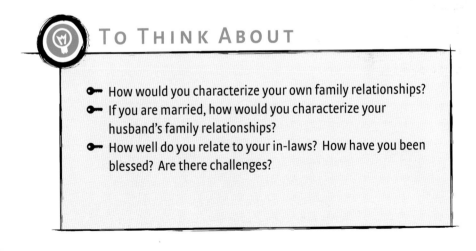

TO THINK ABOUT

- How would you characterize your own family relationships?
- If you are married, how would you characterize your husband's family relationships?
- How well do you relate to your in-laws? How have you been blessed? Are there challenges?

LESSON FOR LIFE

Promises

God will:

Guide you
John 10:27

Bless peacemakers
Matthew 5:9

Use life to build
character
Romans 5:4
James 1:2-4

A Little Loving Kindness

BIBLE STUDY PASSAGE: 1 THESSALONIANS 2:1-13

*But we were very gentle with you, like a mother caring
for her little children.*

1 THESSALONIANS 2:7

Some relationships come so easily and are so healthy and
affirming, while with others, we struggle to connect. Maybe we
aren't in a state of open hostility, but affection and love are
hard to give or receive.

What causes difficult relationships? The list is endless and
can relate to both you and others. Different points of view.
Competition. Self-centeredness. Bad first impressions.
Inability to communicate effectively.

Paul, who most scholars believe was single and never had
in-laws, still knew something about challenging relationships.
He writes to the church in Thessalonica as if they were his own
children. He describes his ministry to them in intimate and
highly relational language. His concern was that they be
strong in their newfound faith and he didn't want any form of
relationship conflict to undermine his teaching. He well under-

stood the saying: People don't care how much you know until they know how much you care.

So Paul's approach to them was as gentle as a mother caring for her child (v. 7). His motives were pure and he never tried to manipulate them (v. 3). His goal was not to be praised but to please God (v. 6). He wasn't a burden to them (v. 6), but loved and delighted in them (v. 7). As a great father deals with his children, Paul encouraged, comforted, and challenged them to lives worthy of God's call on them (vv. 11-12). And, not surprisingly, the people of Thessalonica responded very favorably to Paul's ministry (v. 13).

How wonderful when someone treats us in this way. A teacher. A boss or work colleague. A friend. A parent. An in-law. It's hard to resist such an overflow of love.

Sometimes the people we most desire love and approval from don't express love like Paul did. Instead, they undermine or keep us at a distance. It is then that we, like Paul, must choose first and foremost to please God. Then, whether or not our efforts succeed, we can experience the peace and confidence of doing all we can.

Love is patient and kind.
1 Corinthians 13:4

REAL LIFE

My New Family

ZELNA HARRISON

In the four years I've been married, one of the toughest things for me has been getting along with my in-laws. The love in my husband's family is beyond abundant and the family bond unbelievably close.

So what's the problem?! The day my husband decided to take my hand in marriage, I was told that this family was special and very close-knit, which, in retrospect, seems like an understatement to me. The problem was that I hadn't grown up like that.

I came from a Christian home, but feelings were never shared and the word *love* was rarely, if ever, used in my family. I found interactions with my new family very strange, and it was difficult for me to understand them. This brought confusion and thoughts that my in-laws were the typical overbearing control freaks that have been lampooned in media and jokes.

As a Christian, I thought it would be easy to fit in any family—I never dreamed it would be such a big struggle for me, especially with such nice people. They would ask how my day was, or if there was something that they could do for me. I would immediately think it was their way of keeping an eye on me so that their son was not being neglected. As my feelings of resentment bubbled to the surface, the family thought I did not approve of them. Yet they did not give up—they still showed continuous love toward me.

God knew that my real struggle was being able to accept and give love. He placed me with them knowing that they would help me overcome this challenge. Over these four years, I have come to understand their love for each other, which has helped me to better express my love toward my husband and my children.

Seeing their love has also placed in me a longing to make right some of the things that went wrong in my own family. I can sincerely say that God is helping me grow, even though it is still sometimes difficult for me to express my feelings towards my parents. I now sometimes shyly whisper to my mother that I love her. I can even say that I forgive my father for walking out on us.

I can also say that through my in-laws, I learned what Godly love is, how to accept it, and how to show it.

Sometimes when I sit in the midst of my new family and listen to their happy, light conversation, I'm reminded that I'm blessed and that God knew why He put me and my husband together—for He chose not only my husband, but my in-laws as well.

ACTION STEP

WRITE A LETTER TO YOUR IN-LAWS—OR A SIGNIFICANT RELATIONSHIP IN YOUR LIFE, IF YOU'RE NOT MARRIED—EXPRESSING YOUR LOVE AND GRATITUDE FOR THEM. IF THE RELATIONSHIP IS STRAINED, FIND WAYS TO BUILD BRIDGES OF RECONCILIATION AND FRIENDSHIP.

PRAYER

Thank You for being my God and my Friend. Thank You for the people You have brought into my life. May we grow closer together as we grow closer to You.

AGING WITH GRACE

EVERY SEASON OF LIFE HAS ITS OWN CHALLENGES AND JOYS, AND WE ARE TO SAVOR THEM WITH FAITH AND ENTHUSIASM.

You are as young as your faith, as old as your doubt; as young as your self-confidence, as old as your fear; as young as your hope, as old as your despair.

DOUGLAS MACARTHUR

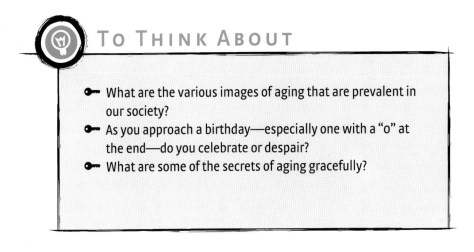

TO THINK ABOUT

- What are the various images of aging that are prevalent in our society?
- As you approach a birthday—especially one with a "o" at the end—do you celebrate or despair?
- What are some of the secrets of aging gracefully?

LESSON FOR LIFE

Promises

God will:

Preserve your health
Exodus 23:25

Satisfy your soul
Psalm 107:9

Sustain the sick
Psalm 41:3

Guide you and
strengthen you
Isaiah 58:11

Seize the Day

BIBLE STUDY PASSAGE: 2 CORINTHIANS 5:1-10

God richly gives us everything to enjoy.

1 TIMOTHY 6:17

Walk into any bookstore, pick up any popular cultural magazine off a news rack, and you will quickly be reminded of how significant an issue aging is to millions of people. Questions abound:

Am I making enough money to secure a comfortable future? What will I do after I retire? Am I in the right career now? How are my kids doing? What kind of world awaits them? How am I doing health-wise? Will I be active and strong after retirement? How do I keep my mind sharp and alert?

Improved healthcare, diet, and other medical and socio-logical factors mean that people today live much longer than at any other moment in history—at least since the early Old Testament record of pre-Flood characters like Methuselah!

Questions of aging aren't just asked by the "old"—and "old" is a very hard concept to define—and not just regarding matters of health and money. Though we appear to be aging

174

more slowly, millions of young adults are already concerned with age issues in regard to attractiveness, career status, and other issues.

The good news is that God has given us everything we need to enjoy life now. Yes, we should plan for and look to the future—the Apostle Paul describes with great emotion how he yearns to be present with Jesus in Heaven (See 2 Corinthians 5:1-10), but the real secret of aging with grace is how you live today.

If you want to increase your chances of being healthy at age eighty, take care of your body with reasonable exercise and diet today. If you want your mind to be sharp and quick in twenty years, read, think, and discuss matters today. If you want to be stronger spiritually in the future and leave a lasting legacy through the people you have touched with grace, then pray and minister today.

Ultimately, the question of how to age gracefully is no different than the question of how to live each day gracefully. Seize the day and enjoy it and live it fully.

Even when you are old, I will be the same. Even when your hair has turned gray, I will take care of you. I made you and will take care of you. I will carry you and save you.

Isaiah 46:4

REAL LIFE

Life—What a Ride!

BETTY KING

Sometimes you have to work at having fun. It had been some time since I had been to a carnival, and this time would be more of a challenge than the carnival visits of my youth.

There's nothing quite like doing something new and different to cause you to feel that thrill and excitement down deep in the pit of your stomach. I've done a few things since I reached my golden years that have caused that adventurous spirit to swell up and explode within me—aerobic glider plane rides, horseback riding in the mountains, a mystery train ride. I could go on and on; life is just a thrill away! Happiness is truly what we make it. We can be happy without the thrill of adventure, but exciting activities increase the pleasure of our journey.

God gave us life, so make the most of the time you're given. Increase your happiness by doing something different; dare yourself to have fun—these had always been my mottos.

And so I told my husband, Bill: "I am not leaving this carnival until I ride on one of these rides."

I knew it would be quite a feat to get me on any ride—carnivals are not generally equipped for people with handicaps. But the only handicap I was experiencing at that point, besides my multiple sclerosis, was my family. I just needed a little help to get on a ride!

Bill thought I was kidding. He finally caught on that I was serious.

"Okay, which one do you want to ride?"

"The Wipe Out!"

While Bill went to purchase my ticket, I asked the fellow operating the ride if I could enter through the exit ramp; it was closer to get to the seat. He looked at me rather sheepishly—me on my three-wheel scooter.

Well, it took effort, I must say, to have fun that evening—but some things are worth the effort! It took Bill, my son Rodney, two canes, the carnival fellow operating the ride, and myself to lift, drag and maneuver me up and around and into that ride. But I made it!

The operator revved up the engines, and my thrill began!

WOW! WHAT A RIDE!

Someone once said, "Life is not a journey to the grave with the intention of arriving safely in a pretty and well-preserved body, but rather to skid in broadside, thoroughly used up, totally worn out, and loudly proclaiming WOW! What a ride!"

That's how I want to live my life. I want to experience the thrill of every moment. I want to know I have completed my life using all that I have, enjoying this journey that God has allotted me.

How about you?

ACTION STEP

WHETHER YOU ARE 10, 30, 70, OR 100 YEARS OLD, ONE SECRET OF LIVING LIFE WELL IS TO HAVE GOALS AND PURPOSE. WRITE OUT A FEW LISTS:

- FIVE THINGS YOU'D LIKE TO EXPERIENCE OR ACCOMPLISH THIS YEAR
- FIVE THINGS YOU'D LIKE TO EXPERIENCE OR ACCOMPLISH IN THE NEXT TEN YEARS
- FIVE THINGS YOU'D LIKE TO EXPERIENCE OR ACCOMPLISH BEFORE YOU DIE

PRAYER

HEAVENLY FATHER, THANK YOU FOR ALL THE OPPORTUNITIES YOU HAVE GIVEN ME TO LIVE A FULL AND RICH LIFE. HELP ME TO LIVE EACH DAY WITH FAITH, GRACE, AND OPTIMISM.

KINDNESS

WE CHANGE THE WORLD ONE PERSON AT A TIME BY THE WAY WE TREAT EACH PERSON WE MEET.

Too often we underestimate the power of a touch, a smile, a kind word, a listening ear, an honest compliment, or the smallest act of caring, all of which have the potential to turn a life around.

LEO BUSCAGLIA

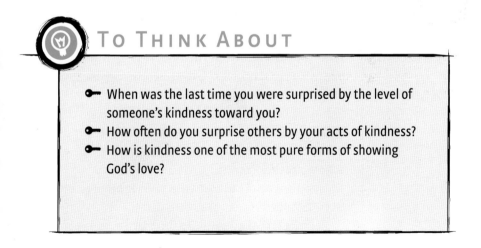

TO THINK ABOUT

- When was the last time you were surprised by the level of someone's kindness toward you?
- How often do you surprise others by your acts of kindness?
- How is kindness one of the most pure forms of showing God's love?

LESSON FOR LIFE

Promises

God will:

Produce kindness in you

Galatians 5:22

Bless others through

your kindness

Proverbs 16:15

Bring people to Himself

through His kindness

Romans 2:4

A Good Neighbor

BIBLE STUDY PASSAGE: LUKE 10:25-37

This is what the Lord All-Powerful says: "Do what is right and true. Be kind and merciful to each other."

ZECHARIAH 7:9

Some religious leaders challenged Jesus with a question about who we should consider as a neighbor. In other words, who was acceptable and who was unacceptable in their highly segregated society?

Jesus gave them an answer, but not to the question they asked. Instead of telling them who their neighbor is, He told them what a good neighbor looks like through the powerful story of the Good Samaritan.

Note, many Jewish leaders of Jesus' day would have nothing to do with Samaritans, so you can imagine how mad they were that Jesus made a Samaritan the hero of the story—and the model for kindness.

In taking care of a fellow traveler who had been beaten and robbed, the Samaritan teaches us that–

• Kindness can be costly—"The next day, the Samaritan

brought out two coins, gave them to the innkeeper, and said, 'Take care of this man. If you spend more money on him, I will pay it back to you when I come again' " (Luke 10:35). No question, kindness requires effort—and sometimes even sacrifice on our part.

- Kindness can be risky—"Evil people will not learn to do good even if you show them kindness" (Isaiah 26:10). Just as the Samaritan man risked being mugged himself by slowing down to help, at times our kindness will be taken advantage of.
- Kindness turns enemies into friends—"The Samaritan went to him, poured olive oil and wine on his wounds, and bandaged them. Then he put the hurt man on his own donkey and took him to an inn where he cared for him" (Luke 10:34). If this Jew and Samaritan could be united through kindness, what might happen to your relationships as you become a good neighbor?
- Kindness saves people's lives—"A smiling king can give people life; his kindness is like a spring shower" (Proverbs 16:15). There are teenage girls, divorcees, senior citizens who have all but given up on a good God because of how they've been treated. You can change their perspective with kindness.

Don't ever forget kindness and truth. Wear them like a necklace. Write them on your heart as if on a tablet.
Proverbs 3:3

181

REAL LIFE

My American Angel

RENIE BURGHARDT

I was fourteen when I boarded the old Navy ship, the U.S.N.S. General M.B. Stewart, in the port of Bremen, Germany. I was with my grandparents, who raised me, and hundreds of other people who were fortunate enough to have been accepted to immigrate to America. World War II had torn apart our lives and displaced us, making us refugees, but our hopes and dreams for a new life soared as we began our journey to America. It was the answer to our prayers.

Crossing the Atlantic took ten days, most in raging, stormy seas. But our arrival on that September day made the journey worthwhile. I remember gazing into the dark distance, entranced by the trillions of lights on the black horizon. It was like a fairyland. Later, as we pulled into the harbor and heard the Star Spangled Banner over the loudspeakers, tears filled our eyes. We had really arrived.

After several hours of processing, we were finally released to our sponsor, Mr. Levin, and his wife, who took us by train to Indiana. During our long train ride, I answered Mrs. Levin's questions in my broken English, painfully aware of my shabby condition and my threadbare clothes. But her gentle ways and bright smile were comforting. In Indiana, Mrs. Levin helped us settle in, and came by to talk to me a few days later. "You'll be going to school soon, so tomorrow you and I are going shopping," she said, smiling at me. "How old did you say you are?"

"I'm almost fifteen," I replied shyly.

"Well, I was thinking that a young lady of almost fifteen might like to get rid of her braids, so we'll visit a beauty shop, too." Her voice was so kind that I had the urge to hug her.

The following day, under Mrs. Levin's guidance, I was transformed. I got a stylish new haircut and new American clothes and shoes. Then she took me to see my first movie, where I got a further boost to my adolescent self-confidence when two teenaged boys made "goo-goo eyes" at me in the lobby. At least that's what Mrs. Levin said they were doing. I blushed, but was secretly pleased about it all.

Over the next few months, she shared many other insights and helped this shy young Hungarian girl blossom into a self-confident young American woman. She was my kind American angel. I have never forgotten the impact of Mrs. Levin's kindness, and have in turn, tried to always be kind to others, praying, *Lord, help me remember always what a big difference a kind smile, an encouraging word, or a visit to someone alone, can make.*

ACTION STEP

A MOVEMENT THAT HAS BEEN QUITE POPULAR IS CALLED RANDOM ACTS OF KINDNESS. THERE WAS EVEN A DAY OF THE YEAR DEDICATED TO GOING ABOVE AND BEYOND IN A LAVISH ACT OF GOODNESS TOWARD OTHERS. THOUGH KINDNESS CAN'T JUST BE FOR A DAY, WE MUST START SOMEWHERE.

PICK A DAY THIS WEEK AND PLOT OUT THREE OR FOUR KIND DEEDS YOU WILL DO FOR FAMILY, NEIGHBORS, AND AT WORK.

PRAYER

God, thank You so much for Your kindness to me, and the kindness shown to me by so many people. Help me be an instrument of Your kindness to someone today.

THE SUPERWOMAN SYNDROME

LIFE IS BUSY AND CHALLENGING, BUT SOME OF THE PRESSURE WE EXPERIENCE COMES FROM OUR OWN UNREALISTIC SELF-EXPECTATIONS.

For disappearing acts, it's hard to beat what happens to the eight hours supposedly left after eight of sleep and eight of work.

DOUG LARSON

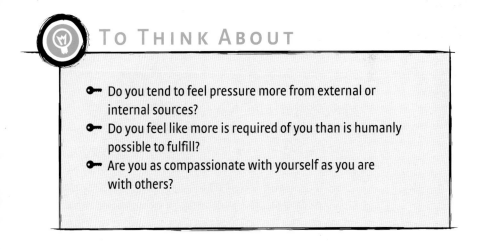

TO THINK ABOUT

- Do you tend to feel pressure more from external or internal sources?
- Do you feel like more is required of you than is humanly possible to fulfill?
- Are you as compassionate with yourself as you are with others?

LESSON FOR LIFE

Promises

God will:

Rejoice over you
Zephaniah 3:17

Bless you
Psalm 5:12

Bring you delight in him
Job 22:21-26

Comfort your anxieties
Psalm 94:19

First Things First

BIBLE STUDY PASSAGE: LUKE 10:38-42

But Martha was busy with all the work to be done. She went in and said, "Lord, don't you care that my sister has left me alone to do all the work? Tell her to help me."

LUKE 10:40

Have you ever found yourself in a situation of being so responsible, so dutiful, so correct in your religious practice that you lost your joy of knowing God?

In the famous parable of the lost son (Luke 15:11-32), a young man rejects his father's teachings and authority, demands his inheritance, and heads for a distant land where he squanders his financial and moral wealth. The loving father never gives up on this prodigal, and when his young son does come to his senses and ashamedly returns home, he welcomes him with open arms. He honors him with a feast, a party, a special cloak, and a golden ring. The older brother, who has faithfully stood by his father's side this whole time, is enraged that the prodigal should receive such a welcome. The father sadly reminds this older son that you don't have to work in a pig sty like his younger brother did to have a piggy attitude. Both sons learn about forgiveness and reconciliation from the love of their father.

In our study passage, we discover that Martha, much like the older brother, holds deep resentment toward a younger sibling. No, Mary is not immoral and rebellious, but she certainly doesn't have Martha's sense of responsibility. She leaves the dishes and chores to her sister so that she can sit at Jesus' feet. Wouldn't you feel a little resentful, too?

Jesus' answer to Martha's demand that He tell Mary to get busy is: "Martha, Martha, you are worried and upset about many things. Only one thing is important. Mary has chosen the better thing, and it will never be taken away from her" (vv. 41-42).

Is Jesus' point that we not care for the maintenance of our homes and families? Of course not. But He does remind us that the heart of our faith, our reason for living, is to love and worship God. Nothing else comes first! And the details of life—those areas in which perfection is elusive even to a Superwoman—are all secondary to our relationship with God.

When You said, "Seek My face," My heart said to You, "Your face, Lord, I will seek."

Psalm 27:8 NKJV

REAL LIFE

Little Answers in Big Places

CAROL HILLEBRENNER

"Something's wrong with Polly today," Marsha complained. "She's in the bathroom crying."

"I'll go see what's wrong."

Polly was sitting on the old vinyl couch in the bathroom near the sanctuary with her back to the door. It looked as if she was napping, until I realized her shoulders were shaking.

"Polly, is there something I can do?"

She shook her head. "Just tired."

I knew that feeling. I sighed and leaned against a stall.

"I said I'd help," Polly sniffed. "I volunteer for everything. I can't say no. I mean," she turned around and looked at me, "I really want to help people, but with my part-time job and the kids and—Jo, are you crying?"

I whipped a tissue from my pocket and dabbed my eyes. "No, just tired. I was up late making Molly's costume for the school play, which I should have done last week, but my job at the museum is nearly full time this month and there was the cookie bake for play rehearsal here at church and—"

"You can't say no either."

I nodded. "And worse, I never get things done as well as I want because something else needs to be done."

"You're a lot of comfort," Polly said with half a smile. We talked and cried some more about wanting to be there for people who needed us and letting our responsibilities pile up—and feeling guilty when we said no.

"What are you two, the sob sisters?" Lavonne asked as she passed between us on her way to a stall.

"Just tired," Polly said again and arose. Signaling me to follow her, she led me into our huge old sanctuary.

Polly sat down, bowing her head in prayer. I joined her, but my silent prayers didn't seem to help.

"Sometimes God's answer is no."

We both jumped at the sound of the voice and looked around. We were alone, but the door above the confirmation room was open and I knew sound carried well from down there when it was quiet in the sanctuary. We looked at each other in astonishment. We both had to stifle giggles because we knew you aren't supposed to laugh when God speaks to you!

"So how do we know when God's saying no?" Polly whispered.

I didn't know. The only thing I knew to do when I was feeling overwhelmed was make lists.

Suddenly an idea hung over me like the proverbial light bulb shining in the darkness of my thoughts. "Have you ever met someone you knew would be good on a committee or someone who seemed interested in doing a project, but you didn't remember them until it was over?"

"Lots of times."

"That's the answer."

"Huh?"

"We can make lists of people who would do things and, when someone calls us to do something, give them the names of people who would really like to take a turn. And if we can't think of anyone, maybe God is saying yes."

"I could say no without feeling guilty."

I nodded and smiled. So did Polly. Our guilt was relieved by figuring out a way to help when help was needed—and by recognizing that we can't be all things to all people. We basked in the rest of the sanctuary for a few minutes before heading back into our busy days.

 ## ACTION STEP

ARE YOU EXPERIENCING THE JOY OF THE LORD IN YOUR LIFE RIGHT NOW? DOES LOVING GOD COME FIRST? THE NEXT TIME YOU FEEL OVERWHELMED BY THE VARIOUS DEMANDS IN YOUR LIFE, ACT COUNTERINTUITIVELY BY STOPPING RIGHT THAT SECOND AND TAKING A MOMENT TO PRAISE AND WORSHIP YOUR LOVING HEAVENLY FATHER.

 ## PRAYER

Turn my heart and mind to You right now, O God, my kind and gracious Lord. I put You before all other relationships, all other tasks.

SIMPLIFYING LIFE

SIMPLICITY PROVIDES EMOTIONAL AND SPIRITUAL FREEDOM FROM THE PRESSURES OF BUSYNESS AND CONSUMERISM.

Simplicity, clarity, singleness: these are the attributes that give our lives power and vividness and joy.

RICHARD HALLOWAY

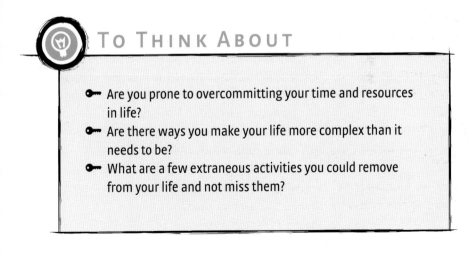

TO THINK ABOUT

- ☞ Are you prone to overcommitting your time and resources in life?
- ☞ Are there ways you make your life more complex than it needs to be?
- ☞ What are a few extraneous activities you could remove from your life and not miss them?

LESSON FOR LIFE

Promises

God will:

Bless you
Psalm 127:1-2

Meet all your needs
Philippians 4:19
Matthew 6:33

Fulfill your desires as
you seek him
Psalm 37:4

Give assurance
of His love
1 John 4:18
Romans 5:5

He Must Become Greater

BIBLE STUDY PASSAGE: JOHN 3:22-30

The thing you should want most is God's kingdom and doing what God wants. Then all these other things you need will be given to you.

MATTHEW 6:33

Popular culture guru Faith Popcorn claims that 80 percent of Americans believe life is too hectic and want to simplify. Evidence of the complexity we build into our lives abounds—

- *We make more money than any other time in history—but have racked up trillions of dollars in personal debt.*
- *We provide every activity and comfort our children could ask for—and they are less satisfied than ever.*
- *We have the most sophisticated computers and business tools—but spend more time at work.*
- *We chase after new purchases—but complain that our homes and closets are cluttered.*

There are a number of steps that go into simplifying life,

but you must always begin by believing that you can live more richly having less—and then making a commitment to that belief. Then, you must determine what is really important to you and make a list of your values. Next you need to honestly assess where your time and money go in light of those values. And finally, you must be persistent in creating a healthier lifestyle.

A word of caution is that we are not all called to simplify in any set way. That frees us from judging others and feeling guilty that we aren't more like others.

What really matters for all of us is that simplicity ultimately is a spiritual issue—a matter of the soul. The key question is whether we have allowed activities, possessions, status, hobbies, entertainment, careers, and other pursuits to come before our love for God—and our relationships with others.

John the Baptist made a powerful statement when pointing to Jesus Christ as the long-awaited Messiah: "He must increase, but I must decrease" (John 3:30). Is Jesus increasing in your life? Is the pull and allure of other things decreasing?

> Think only about the things in heaven, not the things on earth.
> Colossians 3:2

 REAL LIFE

Simplify to Magnify

JOANNE SCHULTE

When I accepted an invitation to a pre-holiday "special day for women," I had no idea the event would alter both my attitude and my plans for the holidays.

The summer heat had finally yielded to autumn's cooler days and crisp, clear nights. With it had come renewed energy and creativity. It arrived not a moment too soon, for the holidays were just around the corner and there was much to be done. There were dinner parties, cookie baking, shopping, decorating, Christmas cards .... The list was endless, but I was ready and eager to tackle them all.

Awakening to a picture-perfect morning, I was excited to see just what this "special day for women" was all about. As I stood up, though, I realized that I was getting a migraine headache. I hadn't had a migraine in years and wondered what my body was trying to tell me with this one.

Why a migraine and why today of all days? Have I been overdoing it? I don't feel tired or stressed. Am I? Have I been burning the candle at both ends without knowing it? Should I cut back a little—not do so much over the holidays? I don't want to get sick. What's going on?

I reached for my migraine medication and waited for my friends. Within a few moments, a van full of chatting and laughing women arrived. As we drove, their festive mood gradually lifted my own spirits.

We entered the building and were soon shopping at a large boutique full of beautiful jewelry, clothing, and home accessories. In the next room we enjoyed a delicious luncheon, beautiful music, door prizes, and a fashion show of holiday outfits. The day was lovely. No, it was more than lovely. It was wonderful. The holiday plans that swirled in my head these past few weeks seemed to have vanished as I relaxed and enjoyed all that was happening around me. It occurred to me that my headache was gone and I was feeling great.

Next came the speaker—a beautiful woman with a thought-provoking message filled with scripture and clothed in humor. One particular thing she said impacted me immediately: "Simplify the season so you can magnify the Savior."

I thought of the long list of things I wanted to do in the next few days.

How could I magnify the Savior if I were exhausted or sick? How important were my plans anyway? Would the holidays be just as nice if I scaled back—simplified?

Because of what I had just heard, my holiday plans were soon changed. A fancy Thanksgiving dinner would be superseded by easy-to-prepare family favorites. We would not have a big Christmas party. No new commitments would be accepted until January. And most importantly, in the days ahead, I would simplify the season, so I could focus on and magnify the Savior.

ACTION STEP

ARE YOU READY TO LIVE MORE BY HAVING LESS?

- CLEAN OUT CLOSETS AND GARAGE AND MAKE A TRIP TO GOODWILL, THE SALVATION ARMY, OR ANOTHER COMPASSIONATE MINISTRY TO MAKE A DONATION. OR PLAN A GARAGE SALE AND PAY OFF ONE OF YOUR BILLS WITH THE PROCEEDS.
- IS THERE AN ACTIVITY IN YOUR LIFE THAT DEMANDS MUCH BUT GIVES LITTLE IN RETURN? CAN YOU ELIMINATE THIS NOW?
- MAKE A LIST OF YOUR CORE VALUES. ASK YOURSELF IF YOUR LIFESTYLE MATCHES YOUR VALUES.

PRAYER

You desire a simple relationship of love and trust with me. Help me to model all of my relationships and life with that sense of simplicity.

LONELINESS

EVEN IF OTHERS FAIL OR DESERT US, GOD IS ALWAYS PRESENT IN OUR LIVES.

Before us is a future all unknown, a path untrod;
Beside us a friend well loved and known—
That friend is God.

AUTHOR UNKNOWN

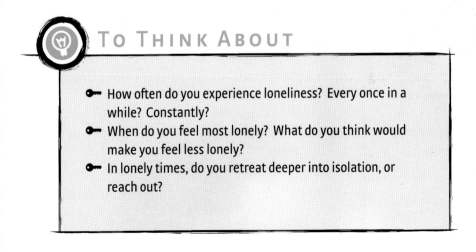

TO THINK ABOUT

- How often do you experience loneliness? Every once in a while? Constantly?
- When do you feel most lonely? What do you think would make you feel less lonely?
- In lonely times, do you retreat deeper into isolation, or reach out?

LESSON FOR LIFE

Promises

God will:

Bring you contentment
Philippians 4:11-13

Provide not just physical
needs, but enjoyment
needs as well
1 Timothy 6:17
2 Peter 1:3

Take on your concerns
Isaiah 49:16

Never leave you
Deuteronomy 31:6

You Are My Friend

BIBLE STUDY PASSAGE: JOHN 15:1-17

Remain in me, and I will remain in you. A branch cannot produce fruit alone but must remain in the vine. In the same way, you cannot produce fruit alone but must remain in me.

JOHN 15:4

In *The Lonely Crowd,* a classic book written by Harvard's David Riesman, he discusses the reality that though we will bump into more people in a week than people during the Middle Ages saw in a lifetime, millions of people are still disconnected and lonely.

Feelings of disconnect can happen after a divorce or extended illness or move to a new city. But maybe you've found yourself lonely at work, in your neighborhood, or even in your church and home.

In some cases just a little initiative, persistence, and patience is all you need to reconnect with the world. For some forms of loneliness—like sleeping alone after years of marriage—we must turn to Jesus, who is the closest and most faithful Friend any person could ever have.

But how is that possible? I need flesh and blood presence in my life. Jesus describes His friendship to His disciples in John 15. He declares that He will always be beside them (15:4); that He will hear their requests and answer them (15:7); that He will enrich their lives and make them fruitful (15:8); that He loves them as God the Father loves Him (15:9); that He will make them joyful (15:11); that He loves them so much he will lay down His life for them (15:13); that He will always perceive them as friends, not servants (15:15); that He chose them as friends, and not the other way around (15:16).

What greater friend could you have? Yes, it's true we need the love and affection of others in our lives, but it's wonderful to know that Jesus will always be the Friend we need.

One thing I have desired of the Lord, That will I seek: That I may dwell in the house of the Lord All the days of my life, To behold the beauty of the Lord, And to inquire in His temple.

Psalm 27:4 NKJV

 REAL LIFE

Eating Peanut Butter with Jesus

EDNA ELLISON

I had just ended an engagement to the wealthiest man in two counties. The day he asked for his ring back, I reluctantly gave it to him and watched that two-carat, $8,000 diamond go out the door. A few weeks later, a friend stopped by my desk at work. "Hey, girl, you look a little down in the mouth. How about a smile for an old friend?"

I smiled. "Sara," I said, "Do you know the worst part of being 'disengaged'?"

"So that's why you're blue," she said. "Is it un-engaged or disengaged?"

I laughed. "Either way, it's not good. The worst part of being disengaged is eating at home alone every night. I miss his wining and dining me at fancy restaurants. We had filet mignon, chicken in wine sauce, key lime pie, chocolate—"

"Hold it!" Sara interrupted. "That's enough of that kind of talk. What are you eating now?"

"Instead of that rich food, I eat a dry peanut butter sandwich at home every night. My budget is tight after buying new clothes to impress him. Now I can't eat out. Peanut butter's cheap; but the more I eat, the dryer that peanut butter sandwich seems."

A divorcee, Sara shared: "Edna, after Charles left us, I was lonely, too. I spent a few nights alone, eating boring meals, but one day my pastor's wife dropped by. She ate a sandwich with me and gave me a little card. Do you know Revelation 3:20?"

"Uh, sure," I said. "I memorized that years ago; let's see—'Behold I stand at the door and knock, and if anyone hears my voice and opens the door, I will come in.'"

"Yes," she said, "but you left off the best part of that verse: 'I will come in and sup with you.'" Sara beamed, her white teeth gleaming. "I have supper with Jesus every night!"

With Sara's help, I began having supper with Jesus every night. Following her example, I set an extra place at the table each night. I put out my finest china and silver. I set my Bible above my plate, with uplifting verses open. One night I remembered the words I'd heard at a women's conference: "If no man ever puts his arms around you and tells you he loves you, remember this: You are a part of the Church, the bride of Christ. He's your Bridegroom. You can lean on his everlasting arms. Nothing you can ever do will make Him stop loving you."

Slowly, I found I could replace my ho-hum meals with an exciting spice of life. I experienced the va-va-va-voom of Jesus! Every day brings a cause for celebration: a pink sunset, a new purse, a cheerful letter, a leaf outside my window. I now celebrate the little things with Christ.

ACTION STEP

ARE THERE FRIENDS AND ACQUAINTANCES IN YOUR LIFE GOING THROUGH A PERIOD OF LOSS AND PAIN? A DIVORCE? A CHILD WHO HAS MOVED OUT ON HIS OR HER OWN? A NEW PERSON IN YOUR CITY? ONE OF THE LOST GRACES IS THAT OF ENTERTAINING. INVITE THAT PERSON OVER TO SHARE A MEAL—OR TAKE THEM OUT FOR DINNER.

PRAYER

I will rejoice in You, O God, as my Savior and Friend. Thank You for always being present in my life.

FREEDOM FROM FEAR

THE ANTIDOTE TO A SUFFOCATING, STIFLING, STAGNATING FEAR IS SIMPLE FAITH.

*You block your dream when you allow your fear
to grow bigger than your faith.*

MARY MANIN MORRISSEY

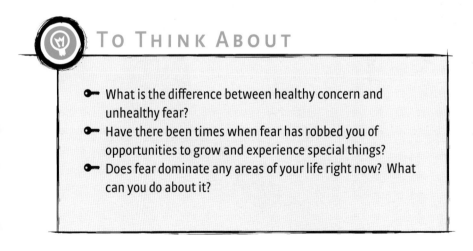

TO THINK ABOUT

- What is the difference between healthy concern and unhealthy fear?
- Have there been times when fear has robbed you of opportunities to grow and experience special things?
- Does fear dominate any areas of your life right now? What can you do about it?

LESSON FOR LIFE

Promises

God will:

Help you in trouble
Psalm 46:1-2

Provide your needs and
give you peace
Philippians 4:6-7

Eliminate fear
Leviticus 26:6

Give boldness
Proverbs 28:1

Baby Steps

BIBLE STUDY PASSAGE: PHILIPPIANS 4:4-7

Jesus said, "Come." And Peter left the boat and walked on the water to Jesus.

MATTHEW 14:29

Nothing can rob you of joy, confidence, optimism, and opportunities more quickly than a spirit of fear.

Behavioral scientists have long debated whether the first emotion a baby experiences is love or fear. Because of the "startle reflex," many researchers believe it is the latter.

When faced with danger, the two foundational responses that appear to be "hard-wired" into the human psyche are fight or flight. So are you a fight or a flight person?

There are many sources of fear. Some are unreasonable (to everyone else but the persons experiencing them!), and are considered unhealthy phobias. But whatever the source—a sense of the unknown, the future, physical danger, spiritual warfare, financial crises, or reputation issues—fear is real and must be faced honestly.

One of the greatest promises of God is that we don't have to face our fears alone. He is always with us; never will He forsake us (Hebrews 13:5). In fact, when we truly experience His love, fear is cast away (1 John 4:18). Why? Love is what must be present for trust to flourish. So remember, if you fear—

- *the past, God makes all things new (2 Corinthians 5:17);*
- *the future, God has promised you a future and a hope (Jeremiah 29:11);*
- *enemies, God will protect and keep you (Deuteronomy 31:6);*
- *financial problems, God will provide for your every need (Philippians 4:19);*
- *death and dying, God has conquered the power of death and promises eternal life (Romans 8:1-2).*

Are you ready to walk boldly, with a new sense of confidence today? Take a few steps, even if they're baby steps, toward God and let Him handle all the anxieties that trouble you.

So don't worry, because I am with you. Don't be afraid, because I am your God. I will make you strong and will help you; I will support you with my right hand that saves you.

Isaiah 41:10

 REAL LIFE

Beauty in the Storm

SUE REEVE

Ominous storm clouds gathered on the horizon as we increased elevation. This wasn't the predicted forecast we heard prior to leaving our house in Coeur d'Alene, Idaho this December morning. My husband Ron and I considered turning back and canceling our quick trip over the Cascade Mountains to attend my sister's surprise landmark birthday party.

Filled with a can-do spirit, Ron insisted we travel on. With the plop of each huge new snowflake, I became more aware of the hazardous road conditions. Ron's obvious enjoyment of this opportunity to try out the car's four-wheel drive capabilities annoyed me. My sense of adventure gave way to concern and tension mounted and muscles tightened as we traveled into the storm.

What if Ron is driving too fast for conditions? He should slow down! What if we slide off the road and down the mountainside? Perhaps we should go back home and call my sister this evening with our well wishes.

"Why don't you stop *what-if*-ing and *should*-ing, sit back, and focus on the journey rather than your fears," a still, small voice within suggested. Then I fixed my eyes to look—truly look—at the magnificent gift of the present.

As we journeyed deeper into the storm, the beauty became more exquisite. Anxious thoughts turned into wondrous exclamations. "Have you ever seen such gigantic snowflakes? These trees look like they've been adorned with extravagant amounts of white puff paint!"

Anxiety decreased as wonder and appreciation increased. "Isn't God's gift of creation amazing?" I marveled. "Can you believe this beauty? Just think what we would've missed if we'd turned back!"

Before long, we reached the mountain pass summit. As we descended the mountain, snowflakes softened, becoming delicate, eventually turning into soft raindrops. Soon we were laughing and hugging my flabbergasted sister.

Pondering this trip through the storm, I recognize the parallels in my life. How often have I retreated cautiously when encountering the possibility of a personal storm? In the middle of an uncomfortable situation, do I fret rather than breath deeply, relax and travel on with confidence? How many serendipitous moments have I missed because I turned back rather than pressing on? How many of God's special gifts have remained unopened because I was *what-if*-ing or *should*-ing?

Now over fifty, I have no plans to become a storm chaser. I will continue to live life practicing prudent caution. The mountain experience, however, kindled a desire to live more fully, approaching life's storms with greater confidence. I desire to use the resources God gives, travel forward, and discover exquisite beauty, even during life's troublesome storms. I want to press on, savor, and see—truly see—the hand of God in each new day.

ACTION STEP

BRENDAN FRANCIS SAYS, "MANY OF OUR FEARS ARE TISSUE-PAPER-THIN, AND A SINGLE COURAGEOUS STEP WOULD CARRY US CLEAR THROUGH THEM."

WHAT IS ONE FEAR YOU ARE LIVING WITH TODAY—AND WHAT IS ONE STEP YOU CAN TAKE TO BREAK THROUGH IT? DETERMINE A STEP THAT YOU CAN CARRY OUT WITHIN THE NEXT FORTY-EIGHT HOURS.

PRAYER

Your love, Heavenly Father, is ever been present in my life and I will always cling to Your love with faith and trust when I feel fear and anxiety in my life. Thank You for always being close.

LEARNING TO LISTEN

RELATIONSHIP-ENHANCING COMMUNICATION IS A TWO-WAY STREET THAT REQUIRES US TO THINK OF OTHERS AS MUCH AS OURSELVES.

Communication means a sharing together of what you really are.
With the stethoscope of love you listen till you hear the heartbeat of the other.
BARTLETT AND MARGARET HESS

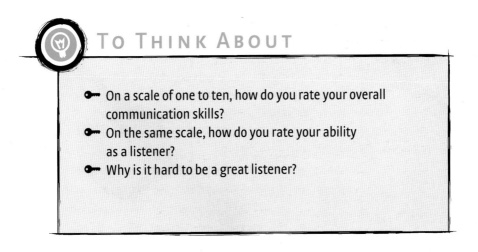

TO THINK ABOUT

- On a scale of one to ten, how do you rate your overall communication skills?
- On the same scale, how do you rate your ability as a listener?
- Why is it hard to be a great listener?

LESSON FOR LIFE

Promises

God will:

Show himself to you as
you seek Him with a
listening heart
1 Chronicles 28:9

Give wisdom
Proverbs 1:23

Use you to bless your
husband
Proverbs 12:4

Watching Our Words Is Hard Work

BIBLE STUDY PASSAGE: PHILIPPIANS 2:5-16

When you do things, do not let selfishness or pride be your guide. Instead, be humble and give more honor to others than to yourselves.

PHILIPPIANS 2:3

We are admonished throughout all of Scripture to watch our words: We are to offer God praise and thanksgiving (Psalm 100:4); we are to treat the name of God with utmost respect (Exodus 20:7); we are to be gentle in the face of anger (Proverbs 15:1); we are to build others up (Ephesians 4:29); we are to avoid profanity and coarse language (Ephesians 5:4); and we are to tell the truth (Exodus 20:16 and 23:1). James says that our words are like the rudder on a ship or a spark that starts a forest fire—they can do great works or cause great damage (3:2-8)!

One other crucial way we are to watch our words is by simply remaining silent and listening to others: "My dear friends, you should be quick to listen and slow to speak or to get angry" (James 1:19 NKJV). If you stop to think about it, listening is actually one of the most powerful expressions of love.

Because listening says to a person: You are important to me; your ideas and feelings matter to me; share your life with me.

We live in a fast-paced, busy, and noisy culture. The TV and radio and other forms of entertainment bombard us from morning to night. Media superstars are referred to as "talking heads." No wonder so many of us feel unheard and underappreciated. Maybe there's no one there to listen to you right now, but you could be there to listen to someone else.

In Philippians 2:4, Paul says to us: "Do not be interested only in your own life, but be interested in the lives of others." The ratio of how much we listen to how much we talk is a pretty good barometer of how much we really look to the interests of others.

Does this mean that you are to be doomed to a life of never sharing what's on your heart and mind? Absolutely not! For in the same way that when we give, we receive back so much more; when we give the gift of a listening ear, others reach out in their hearts to know us better.

My dear brothers and sisters, always be willing to listen and slow to speak.

James 1:19

211

REAL LIFE

Listen and Learn

NANCY C. ANDERSON

I talk much more than I listen. I think I overwhelmed my husband, Ron, with my long-winded descriptions of the perfect pedicure or how hurt I was by our neighbor's sarcastic comments about my new car, and I noticed that Ron didn't talk to me as much as he used to. So I decided to stop prattling on about myself, ask question about his life, and really listen to his answers. My efforts are paying off.

Just the other evening I asked him, "What was the first movie you ever saw in a theater?"

He thought about it for a minute, laughed aloud, and said, "Well—the first time I went to a theater I didn't see the movie; I just saw the bathroom."

I was afraid to ask, but I forged on. "What happened?"

"There was a theater a few doors down from our house in St. Louis, and one summer afternoon I went there with my friends Jimmy Joe, and Skidmark."

I laughed, "Skidmark?"

"Trust me, you don't want to know how he got his nickname. Anyway, the three of us tried to sneak into the theater because we didn't have any money, but the manager saw us lurking near the back door and told us to leave. We were mad at him, so we decided to get back at him. We stood on our tiptoes, peeked into the open bathroom window, and threw in a stink bomb!"

I was a bit disgusted at his behavior, but didn't let it show because Ron was laughing so hard at the memory that he had to stop to catch his breath. "The three of us ran around to the front of the theater," he continued, "and laughed our heads off as we watched the people tumble out of the door, gasping for fresh air."

I was delighted to see Ron so happy about reliving his childhood, so I said, "Tell me another story."

He told me several crazy tales about his unsupervised childhood, and some of the silly—and dangerous—things he did with his cousin Larry. I didn't interrupt him or criticize his youthful tales of reckless antics. I just laughed, smiled, nodded—and listened.

Later that evening when we were lying in bed, he held my hand and said, "You're a good wife." But I think he really meant, "You're a good listener."

I discovered that the more I listened to him, the more I understood him, and the more I understood him, the more he opened up to me. I've learned about his fears, his childhood disappointments and triumphs, and his hopes for the future. We are growing closer each time that I am, as James 1:19 says, "quick to listen and slow to speak."

ACTION STEP

CHOOSE SOMEONE IN YOUR FAMILY OR NEIGHBORHOOD AND SET AS A GOAL THAT YOU ARE GOING TO TRULY GET TO KNOW HIM OR HER BETTER OVER THE NEXT MONTH. FIRST, YOU MUST SET ASIDE ASSUMPTIONS THAT YOU ALREADY KNOW THE PERSON INSIDE AND OUT. SECONDLY, BE PREPARED TO FACE SOME REJECTION. YOUR SPOUSE OR CHILD OR NEIGHBOR MIGHT BE SHOCKED WHEN YOU PURSUE THEM WITH A LISTENING HEART! THIRD, PROVIDE YOUR-SELF WITH A LIST OF CONVERSATION STARTERS TO MAKE THIS ACTIVITY MORE VALUABLE. FINALLY, EVALUATE WHAT YOU LEARN OVER THE NEXT WEEKS. ARE THERE SURPRISES? HOW DID THIS AFFECT YOUR RELATIONSHIP?

PRAYER

God, I come to You today with a quiet and listening heart, ready to hear and follow what You have to say to me.

GRATITUDE

NOTHING WILL CHANGE YOUR PERSPECTIVE
AND ATTITUDE ON LIFE MORE QUICKLY AND
PROFOUNDLY THAN A SPIRIT OF GRATITUDE.

Gratitude is happiness doubled by wonder.

G.K. CHESTERTON

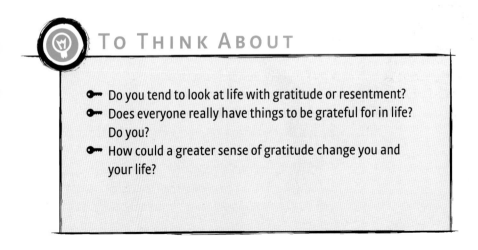

TO THINK ABOUT

- Do you tend to look at life with gratitude or resentment?
- Does everyone really have things to be grateful for in life? Do you?
- How could a greater sense of gratitude change you and your life?

LESSON FOR LIFE

Promises

God will:

Bless you above and
beyond your needs
Psalm 104:14-15

Bring you joy
Psalm 13:5-6

Exceed your expecta-
tions and fill your heart
with His love
Ephesians 3:14-21

Give Thanks

BIBLE STUDY PASSAGE: PSALM 100

Continue praying, keeping alert, and always thanking
God.

COLOSSIANS 4:2

One of the lost arts of civility and friendship is the hand-
written note. It seemingly takes forever to write out a note of
gratitude in a technologically advanced world where we can
tap out a few letters—not necessarily spelled correctly—on
our cell phone or laptop and send an instant message to our
friends and family. But the real tragedy is when we lose our
sense of gratitude for others and for God.

What happens when vibrant, active, kind, fun, difference-
making individuals lose the wonder of gratitude? Almost
overnight you see a change of expression and feel the shrinking
of the soul.

What is the cure for anger, bitterness, resentment, jeal-
ousy, low self-esteem, a quarreling spirit, and other modern
maladies? Simple. Express thanks! Instead of buying into the
advertising of a consumer culture, we need to begin focusing

on what we do have, not what we don't have.

In the one hundredth Psalm, King David leads his people in true worship. They are to honor God with glad hearts and joyful songs. Not only are they to have a thankful attitude, but they must say it aloud and "give thanks." David knows the real reasons for gratitude—

- *We have been created by God and belong to Him (100:3). The world is filled with arrogant people who only acknowledge themselves. But does this attitude really bring contentment and higher levels of self-actualization? It's not possible. Only when we acknowledge God do we discover our true selves.*
- *The Lord is good and His love endures forever (100:5). Does this mean that everything went right for David? Hardly. His life was filled with heartache and disappointment. There were times he lived in a state of depression and near despair. And yet, he understood that even in the "valley of the shadow of death" (Psalm 23:4 NKJV), God was always near to comfort and bless him.*

Nothing will soothe the discomfort you may feel about your financial situation, marital status, or physical attributes like praising God for His goodness and blessings—and knowing that He has blessed you indeed.

Every good action and every perfect gift is from God. These good gifts come down from the Creator of the sun, moon, and stars, who does not change like their shifting shadows.

James 1:17

 REAL LIFE

The Magic Pillow

NANCY B. GIBBS

Valentine's Day had arrived and, like every other day of the year, I was very busy.

My romantic husband, Roy, planned a date like we had never had before. A reservation at an expensive restaurant was made. A beautifully wrapped gift had been sitting on my dresser for a few days prior to the heart-filled holiday.

After a hard day at work, I hurried home, ran into the house, and jumped into the shower. When my sweetheart arrived, I was dressed in my finest outfit and ready to go. He hugged me and smiled. We were both excited.

Unfortunately, the littlest member of our household wasn't so happy.

"Daddy, you were going to take me to buy Mamma a present," Becky, my eight-year-old daughter, said as she sadly walked over to the couch and sat down.

Roy looked at his watch and realized that if we were to make our reservations, we had to leave right away. He didn't even have a few minutes to take her to the corner drugstore, to buy a heart-shaped box of chocolate candy.

"I'm sorry I was late getting home, honey," he said.

"That's okay," Becky replied. "I understand."

I couldn't help being concerned about the disappointment in Becky's eyes. I remembered how the joyful Valentine's Day glow left her face, just before the door closed behind us. She wanted me to know how much she loved me.

Today, I can't remember what was wrapped in that beautiful box, which I swooned over for several days, but I'll never forget the special gift, which I received when we arrived back home.

Becky was asleep on the couch, clutching a box wrapped in newspaper on her lap. When I kissed her cheek, she awoke. "I've got something for you, Mamma," she whispered.

After Roy and I left for our date, Becky had gotten busy. She raided my fabric and cross-stitch box. She stitched the words "I Love Ya" on a piece of red fabric, cut the cloth in the shape of a heart, stitched the two mismatched pieces together, adorned it with lace and stuffed it with cotton. It was a lopsided heart-shaped pillow, filled with love, for which I'll forever be grateful.

My wonderful Valentine gift has a special place in my bedroom today, many years later. As Becky grew into a young woman, many times I held that pillow close to my heart. I don't know if a pillow can hold magic, but this pillow has surely held a great deal of joy for me over the years. It helped me through quite a few sleepless nights after Becky left home for college. I not only cherish the gift, I cherish the memory, as well.

ACTION STEP

GOD GAVE YOU A GIFT OF 86,400 SECONDS TODAY. HAVE YOU USED ONE TO SAY "THANK YOU"?
WILLIAM A. WARD

TAKE TIME TO WRITE SEVERAL THANK YOU NOTES: ONE TO A PERSON FROM YOUR PAST WHO HAS BLESSED YOUR LIFE; ONE TO A FAMILY MEMBER WHO PERHAPS YOU'VE BEEN TEMPTED TO TAKE FOR GRANTED; AND WRITE ONE LETTER TO GOD, THANKING HIM FOR HIS LOVE AND MERCY. TUCK THIS FINAL LETTER IN THE BACK OF YOUR BIBLE FOR FUTURE REFERENCE.

PRAYER

Thank You for who You are and all You have done for me, O God.

THE GIFT OF HOSPITALITY

WHEN YOU OPEN YOUR HEART AND HOME TO FRIENDS, FAMILY, AND ACQUAINTANCES, YOU TRULY MINISTER ON BEHALF OF GOD.

The road to a friend's house is never long.

DANISH PROVERB

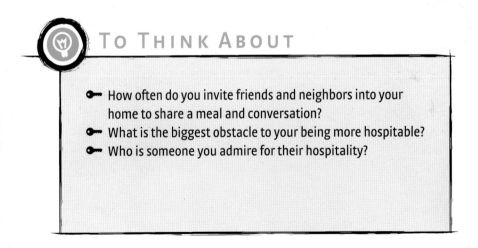

TO THINK ABOUT

- How often do you invite friends and neighbors into your home to share a meal and conversation?
- What is the biggest obstacle to your being more hospitable?
- Who is someone you admire for their hospitality?

LESSON FOR LIFE

You Invited Me In

BIBLE STUDY PASSAGE: MATTHEW 25:31-46

Keep on loving each other as brothers and sisters. Remember to welcome strangers, because some who have done this have welcomed angels without knowing it.

HEBREWS 13:1-2

We wax nostalgic for an age of innocence when neighbors dropped in unannounced and ended up staying for supper, and no one thought anything much of it; when you didn't lock doors at night because you knew all your neighbors by first and last name; when kids played in the street and all the neighborhood congregated to visit out on their front porches.

Today we erect privacy fences so we can sit on our back yards without the prying eyes of neighbors. We click the garage door opener, pull the car quickly inside, and click again for the door to shut without seeing or greeting anyone.

The spirit of hospitality—warmly and generously welcoming guests into our homes—goes back to ancient times and has a fascinating history. The great Hebrew patriarch, Abraham, opened his "home" to strangers, only to discover that they carried an important promise from God (Genesis 14:17-24). Jesus was criticized by the political and religious leaders of his day, for He loved to partake of hospitality—even that of sinners (Matthew 9:10-11).

During early church history and the Middle Ages "hospitality" became nearly synonymous with benevolent service to strangers, often in the form of medical attention, which is where we borrowed the modern Anglo-Saxon word for hospitals.

In a cold, disconnected world, hospitality truly is a healing, restorative act of ministry. It turns strangers into friends. It is a balm for loneliness. It is experiencing friends on a deeper level. It is an opportunity to share food and hearts together.

But my house isn't big enough. My kids always make a mess. I don't have any good recipes. We're so tired by the weekend that I just don't have the energy to open my home.

Hospitality—like waiting for the perfect time to get married or have kids—requires a decision to love others, even when circumstances are less than perfect, by opening your heart and home to them now.

Share with God's people who need help. Bring strangers in need into your homes.
Romans 12:13

REAL LIFE

Something Special in the Dining Room

JOANNE SCHULTE

I could never have imagined how special my luncheon would turn out to be, but I knew it would be different from all I had hosted previously, and I wondered why.

Each of the "young at heart" senior ladies on the guest list thanked me for her invitation and said how much she was looking forward to the day. Although I often entertain, for some reason I was anticipating this event more than most.

When the guests arrived, my house was sparkling clean, and everything about it said, "Welcome." Beautiful china and home grown flowers adorned the table while food waited in the kitchen for the perfect moment to be served.

The chatter of the ladies filled my dining room like a ray of sunshine. Sometimes I would interject a question or comment, but mostly I basked in the pleasure of listening to them talk—getting to know them better in the process. I wondered why I had waited so long to have this luncheon.

Because they were good friends, my guests felt free to talk about the physical and emotional pains they were experiencing, and I realized their beautiful, smiling faces masked hurting hearts and bodies. However, this was not a pity party I was hearing, but a sharing of common experiences, a bonding of lives. From time to time heads nodded as if to say, "I understand." And now and then someone would use her handkerchief to wipe away a tear. It would be difficult to say anything with that lump in my throat, but then nothing needed to be said just now.

After a long pause, one woman bowed her head and prayed out loud for the cares and concerns that had just been expressed. She prayed for only a few moments, but what a difference those few moments made. Time was suspended. Eyes did not open nor did heads look up right away. No one spoke for quite a while, but the looks on their faces said their problems already seemed easier to handle. Their eyes were full of thankfulness and hope. It had been a special moment.

They seemed hesitant to leave, but as they did, each lady hugged me and thanked me—expressing once again just how much she had enjoyed the luncheon.

After I said good-bye to the last guest, I deliberately paused to let the warm glow from the luncheon linger in my thoughts. I doubted any luncheon could ever surpass this one. Those lovely ladies had been my guests. But because I enjoyed them so much, I had the strangest feeling I had been their guest for something special in the dining room—along with Someone very special indeed.

 ## Action Step

INVITE A FAMILY FROM YOUR NEIGHBORHOOD OR CHURCH OVER FOR DINNER.
ASK SOMEONE WHO ISN'T ALREADY A CLOSE FRIEND. IF THIS MAKES YOU A
LITTLE UNCOMFORTABLE, ALLOW GOD TO STRETCH YOU BEYOND YOUR
COMFORT ZONE.

 ## Prayer

Thank You, dear Lord, for loving me when I was a stranger from You. Help me to turn strangers into friends through Your grace and power.

YOUR PARENTS

OUR RELATIONSHIP WITH OUR PARENTS CONTINUES TO BE A SOURCE OF JOY— AND SOMETIMES CHALLENGES— LONG AFTER WE BECOME ADULTS.

You don't choose your family. They are God's gift to you, as you are to them.

DESMOND TUTU

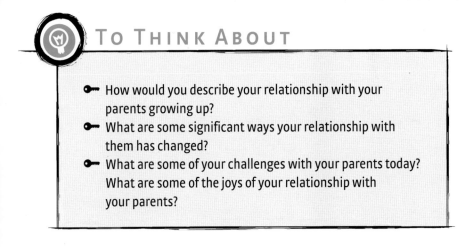

TO THINK ABOUT

- How would you describe your relationship with your parents growing up?
- What are some significant ways your relationship with them has changed?
- What are some of your challenges with your parents today? What are some of the joys of your relationship with your parents?

LESSON FOR LIFE

Promises

God will:

Enrich your life as you
continue to honor your
parents

Exodus 20:12

Reward your persistence
in doing good

Galatians 6:9

Bless your home

Proverbs 3:33

Help you reconcile diffi-
cult relationships

2 Corinthians 5:18

Staying Close to Home

BIBLE STUDY PASSAGE: EPHESIANS 4:29-32

*Be kind and loving to each other, and forgive each other
just as God forgave you in Christ.*

EPHESIANS 4:32

Just because you're an adult doesn't mean your parent or
parents aren't still your parents! For some blessed individuals,
the transition to an adult relationship with parents is smooth,
with natural, easy communication and interaction. Most
adults, though, have at least some difficulty shifting from
dependence to a more equal, though respectful, relationship.
Some of the key issues to resolve include—

- *Letting go of the past: One of the hardest realities of life is that
  our parents aren't perfect. Perhaps you came from a divorced
  home or one that lacked warmth and affection. As an adult,
  you must let go of the past with forgiveness and perspective
  (Philippians 3:13-14).*
- *Dealing openly with current conflicts: Because of respect and
  familiarity, we sometimes struggle to effectively address prob-*

228

lems with those we love most. It is possible to honor your parents and confront disagreements and hurts by "speaking the truth in love" (Ephesians 4:15).

- Accepting your parents for who they are: Just as you may have felt resentment toward your parents for trying to "control" your life, so you must extend the same honor and respect for their opinions, attitudes, and actions that you have desired for yourself. St. Peter said, "Love will cover a multitude of sins" (1 Peter 4:8 NKJV).

- Setting appropriate boundaries: When God instituted marriage, He said, "So a man will leave his father and mother and be united with his wife, and the two will become one body" (Genesis 2:24). Whether or not you are married, God expects you to take responsibility to build your own life. Countless marriages are damaged when priority is placed on parents over spouses. Again, this in no way implies a lack of respect or active honoring of your parents.

- Staying close and expressing love: Even if you must take the lead and be the one to initiate affection, tell and show your parents how much you love them by giving them your time. Don't hold back hugs and "I love yous." Remember, when you are a peacemaker, God blesses you (Matthew 5:9)!

The command says, "Honor your father and mother." This is the first command that has a promise with it—"Then everything will be well with you, and you will have a long life on the earth."
Ephesians 6:2-3

REAL LIFE

Labor of Love

TEENA M. STEWART

A trapped bird beat frantically against the garage window. I'd experienced the same feeling of desperation trying to duplicate healthy mother/daughter bonds.

Mom's insecurities and negative mindset became magnified after my dad died. They became a huge barrier between us. She wasn't a good listener, so our conversations were lopsided as Mom recited her latest ailments blanketed in gloom and doom. I often hung up the phone discouraged. When I married and moved away, the geographical distance mirrored my distant relationship with Mom. I dealt with homesickness, putting up a self-sufficient wall, though I still called home regularly.

One day, after another exasperating "conversation" with my mother, I typed out the issues on paper. But when I prayed over it, I felt God holding me back from mailing the letter. If two previous attempts hadn't persuaded Mom to change, this one wouldn't either. I thought of Proverbs 15:1: "A soft answer turns away wrath." Confrontation wasn't the answer.

Not long after, I shared my frustrations in my women's small group and was surprised to find many had strained relationships with their moms. That day I learned that that no matter how hard I wanted our relationship to be great, it probably never would be.

I couldn't change Mom, but God could change me. I asked Him to help me love her. When I confessed my hurts, God began tearing down the barrier. Slowly,

God gave me wisdom and understanding regarding why my mom was the way she was. I was able to extend grace to her.

I understand now that our experiences and upbringing shape us. Mom was the youngest girl of thirteen children. She had to talk loudly and frequently to be heard among her siblings. Now, when I phone, I know I can't wait for a lull in conversation. I interject what I have to say and steer the conversation. Mom never notices the interruption.

I have also learned to show I care despite my strained relationship. She may find my Christmas and birthday gifts imperfect, but when I act like I love her, it is easier to love her. Sometimes I even share prayer requests with her. It lets her feel needed and breaks down the walls of self-sufficiency I've built.

A few summers ago Mom visited us. Our family drove to the top of Pike's Peak while Mom excitedly snapped photos. When it was time to drive down, she handed me a bag from the gift shop. Inside was a souvenirish necklace of polished black beads—not my taste, but I was touched she took the time to find something just for me.

Right after the 9/11 attacks, Mom called. "I just wanted to make sure you weren't flying anywhere," she said, then proceeded to talk about how she was at the hair dresser's when it all happened and...

The conversation was typical and rambling. Mom hasn't changed. But when I hung up the phone, it hit me: She was calling to hear my voice.

It is good to be loved.

ACTION STEP

A FAVORITE HOBBY FOR MANY FAMILIES IS CREATIVE MEMORY "SCRAP-
BOOKING." FOR THE NEXT SPECIAL OCCASION WHEN YOU WILL SEE YOUR
PARENTS OR A PARENT, PUT TOGETHER A SMALL NOTEBOOK TO "HONOR" YOUR
RELATIONSHIP WITH THEM, FOCUSING ON USING "TOGETHER" PICTURES. YOU
MIGHT MAKE A SECOND NOTEBOOK TO KEEP AT YOUR HOME AS A REMINDER
OF YOUR LOVE FOR THEM!

PRAYER

*Thank You, O God, that as I honor my parents with love and time, You bless
and honor me.*

BEATING THE BLUES

HAVING A RELATIONSHIP WITH GOD DOES NOT MEAN THAT WE WILL NEVER BE DEPRESSED—OR NEED THE SUPPORT OF OTHERS.

*The soul would have no rainbow
had the eyes no tears.*

JOHN VANCE CHENEY

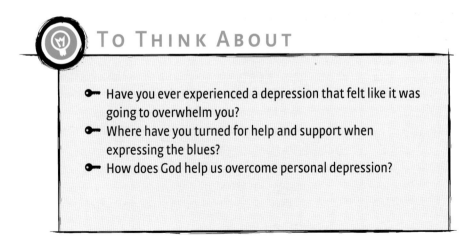

TO THINK ABOUT

- ☛ Have you ever experienced a depression that felt like it was going to overwhelm you?
- ☛ Where have you turned for help and support when expressing the blues?
- ☛ How does God help us overcome personal depression?

LESSON FOR LIFE

Promises

God will:

Continue to bless you
and keep you close to
Him

Jeremiah 32:40

Sustain the sick

Psalm 41:3

Be true to His Word

Isaiah 40:8

Be steadfast

Hebrews 6:19

The Lifter of My Head

BIBLE STUDY PASSAGE: 1 KINGS 19:1-8

Yea, though I walk through the valley of the shadow of death, I will fear no evil; for You are with me; your rod and Your staff, they comfort me.

PSALM 23:4 NKJV

The word "depression" connotes a full range of meanings in our culture, from a quick, temporary feeling of hurt or disappointment, to a state of being physically and emotionally incapacitated by long-term feelings of intense sadness. There are also many ideas as to the sources of depression: lack of appropriate care as children; stress due to significant loss; negative thinking; repressed anger; and a number of biological causes, from injury to hormonal imbalances to nerve damage.

Just as there are multiple sources of depression, so there are multiple ways to receive help:

Physically, you may need—
- Rest .
- Exercise.

234

- Improved dietary habits.

Emotionally, you may need—

- Friends.
- Avoidance of destructive personalities.
- Service opportunities.

Spiritually, you may need—

- More time in God's Word.
- More time in prayer.
- A new understanding of how much God loves you.

Lord, You have heard the desire of the humble; You will prepare their heart; You will cause Your ear to hear.

Psalm 10:17 NKJV

One of the most dramatic stories in the Old Testament was when the prophet Elijah became so distraught that he wanted to die (1 Kings 19:4). He felt he was the only person left who served God. He had obeyed God, but his life was still in danger (1 Kings 19:10). Always be mindful that just as God supernaturally helped Elijah (1 Kings 19:5-8), He is ready to help you.

And also be mindful that God uses others to help His children. Never be ashamed to seek the help of a professional counselor who can help you work through causes of depression in your life.

Know that the day is coming when you can sing with David: "He lifted me out of the pit of destruction, out of the sticky mud. He stood me on a rock and made my feet steady" (Psalm 40:2).

 ## REAL LIFE

So Simple

BOBBI RAUSKY AS TOLD TO JAN WILSON

At first it seemed so harmless and wonderful: open our hearts to two children and adopt them. Like God adopted us into His family. But in the first six months of trying to raise someone else's kids, I saw more raw sewage in my heart than I ever knew was hidden there. Despite raising two other children who grew into healthy adults, I was failing this new challenge miserably.

I felt separated from God, too. Every morning, I'd pray for the grace to be patient and kind with the children. Each evening, when I reviewed my failures during that day, my frustration accumulated. If I can't extend grace to these kids, I thought, how can I ask God to give me grace? How can I ask for His forgiveness, when I can't forgive the hurtful things they do to me? My own thoughts condemned me.

One New Year's Eve I started to think of killing myself. When I pictured my grown daughter finding me, I cringed to think what it would do to her faith. At that moment, I knew I needed help.

Lord, if I can't be happy in this life, I prayed, *please use this situation to make me more like You. Use this to make me holy.*

Midnight drew near and the heaviness lifted slightly. I promised myself to contact a Christian counselor for help with this.

When I started counseling, my emotional EKG was flat. I kept wondering, how did I get so far away from God? And how do I get back?

In the past, the things I read in the Bible seemed to find a place in my heart. Something inside me would leap with joy or relax with peaceful assurance when I read it. But I didn't have any of that now. I approached the Word in a new way, without any feeling. There was no emotional feedback from inside to tell me that something was true or that it applied to me. If I hadn't been so emotionally blank, I probably would have been terrified. With encouragement from the counselor, I continued to read the Bible and pray for the faith to believe the things I could not feel.

Over the coming months, a barely perceptible change took place, which grew and grew. I was learning to accept what the Word says because it is God's Word, whether or not my feelings showed up to echo it.

I wish I could say that before I knew it I was singing "Zip-a-Dee-Doo-Dah," but it just didn't happen that way. In fact, if it did, I would have missed one of the most loving lessons that God ever taught me. Through the painful process of learning to trust God through my depression, I learned that what He says is true and I can stake my life on it. Even when I don't feel a thing.

I still struggle and sometimes fail with the kids, but we are all learning to forgive and move forward.

And now, my faith rests on how reliable He is, not how reliable I am.

ACTION STEP

IS THERE SOMEONE CLOSE TO YOU WHO IS IN THE PIT OF DEPRESSION? HOW CAN YOU APPROPRIATELY REACH OUT TO THAT FRIEND AND PROVIDE PHYSICAL, EMOTIONAL, AND SPIRITUAL SUPPORT? WHAT CAN YOU DO TODAY?

PRAYER

Heavenly Father, when Your children hurt and are in despair, You love as a mother who tends to the needs of a hurting child. Thank You for always being close to me.

OBEDIENCE

THOUGH IT'S SOMETIMES DIFFICULT, WE PLEASE GOD AND LIVE THE LIFE HE INTENDED FOR US WHEN WE CHOOSE TO FAITHFULLY OBEY HIM.

*One act of obedience is better
than one hundred sermons.*

DIETRICH BOENHOEFFER

TO THINK ABOUT

- Have you ever struggled with obedience because it seemed too hard and didn't make perfect sense?
- What are the benefits of obeying God?
- Is there an area of your life where you don't want to obey right now? What will you do about it?

LESSON FOR LIFE

Promises

God will:

Give you joy as you

trust Him

Psalm 33:21

Bless your obedience

Psalm 112:1

Take care of you as you

obey Him

Isaiah 1:19

The Obedience of Mary

BIBLE STUDY PASSAGE: LUKE 1:26-56

Mary said, "I am the servant of the Lord. Let this happen to me as you say!"

LUKE 1:38

Mary, the mother of Jesus, is perhaps the best known of all the women of the Bible—people across the world know who she was and honor her. It was to Mary that God first revealed His specific plan to "save his people from their sins" through her Son (Matthew 1:21).

Mary was an ordinary young woman, engaged to a carpenter named Joseph, until one day, an angel suddenly appeared and said, "Greetings! The Lord has blessed you and is with you" (Luke 1:28), changing her life forever. The angel told her that she had been chosen to carry Jesus, the Savior of the world.

Mary could have asked a lot of questions—"What will Joseph think?" "What will happen to us?" If Mary was thinking these questions, she didn't say so. She never argued or said, "Let me think this over." She simply said yes to God's plan: "Let this happen to me as you say" (Luke 1:38). She placed her reputation, her marriage, and her entire life at risk to be obedient to God—and trusted that His will was perfect.

And because of her trust and obedience, salvation became available to all humanity.

Mary's simple faith and readiness to do God's will brought the blessing of God into her life—and that same faith and obedience will bless your life today.

Obey me, and I will be your God and you will be my people. Do all that I command so that good things will happen to you.

Jeremiah 7:23

REAL LIFE

Miracle in the Making

MELINDA TOGNINI

Every time my daughter smiles, I am overwhelmed with emotion as I am reminded once again that she is the baby who might never have been.

During my pregnancy, a routine ultrasound revealed that our unborn child had severe heart defects. We were told that corrective surgery would probably not be possible, but there were operations that would help her survive. She had a fifty-fifty chance of living to adulthood. Quality of life and life expectancy could not be guaranteed.

We were presented with a grim choice: proceed with the pregnancy or abort.

In some ways, it seemed easier to end it rather than begin to love her and then lose her. But I knew from friends' experiences that grief was difficult no matter when you lost a baby. Besides, she had a small chance. If we terminated the pregnancy, we gave her no chance and we gave God no opportunity to intervene—I would forever wonder, "What if?" There was no question in our minds that God wanted us to keep the baby and trust Him with the outcome.

I cried as we left the hospital. We visited our pastors and cried again. I talked to my family and cried again.

We survived on the prayers and support from family friends—and complete strangers who heard our story. We were told of entire churches full of people who didn't know us personally but were praying for our baby's healing.

During this time, a friend gave me the words of Mark 5:36: "Trust me." In another translation, it read, "Don't be afraid; just believe."

For me, our ordeal came down to these words—trust Me. God was asking us to trust Him and obey. Trust Him that He loved our baby as much as we did, and that He was in control. It required a daily decision to do so, and I wasn't always successful. Some days we felt strong and full of hope. Other days, I couldn't stop crying, as the fear of the unknown overwhelmed me.

On June 21, 2004, after three and a half hours of labor, Alessandra Jayne was born, relatively pink and healthy.

At six days old, our daughter underwent surgery. She was home in six days despite being told she would be in hospital for up to two weeks.

Since then, Alessandra has been an absolute delight to us and to everyone who meets her.

While our journey is far from over, and we face further surgery, I am reminded every day of what God has done so far. An almost non-existent pulmonary artery has developed. A child who could have died has lived so that doctors were able to operate. Corrective surgery may now be possible sometime down the road. God has given me greater contentment with motherhood and deepened my marriage as well.

Alessandra's healing is an ongoing process, but it is nothing less than a miracle. Our miracle is still in the making, and He continues to ask us to trust Him and obey Him as He works it out to completion.

ACTION STEP

SECOND CHRONICLES 7:14 SAYS "THEN IF MY PEOPLE, WHO ARE CALLED BY MY NAME, ARE SORRY FOR WHAT THEY HAVE DONE, IF THEY PRAY AND OBEY ME AND STOP THEIR EVIL WAYS, I WILL HEAR THEM FROM HEAVEN. I WILL FORGIVE THEIR SIN, AND I WILL HEAL THEIR LAND."

WRITE OUT YOUR OWN PRAYER OF HUMBLE REPENTANCE, ASKING GOD TO FORGIVE AREAS OF DISOBEDIENCE AND HELP YOU MAKE ANY CHANGES IN YOUR LIFE THAT NEED TO BE MADE.

PRAYER

Father God, help me remember that Your will is good, pleasing, and perfect. I pray that Your will would be done in my life every day. Help me humbly follow You.

A PRAYER FOR YOUR SOUL

The most important soul matter, of course, is having a relationship with God. Everything in our lives—everything in our entire existence—has new, eternal meaning when we understand that God loves us and has made a way to save us through Jesus Christ. All of this may be new to you. If you'd like to know that you have a lasting relationship with God through Jesus, pray this prayer:

Heavenly Father, I come to You admitting that I am a sinner. I believe that Your Son, Jesus, died on the cross and rose from the dead to take away my sins. Jesus, I choose to follow You and ask that You fill me with the Holy Spirit so that I can understand more about You. Thank You for adopting me, and thank You that I am now a child of God. Amen.

HOW TO READ AND STUDY THE BIBLE

One of the most important keys to nurturing your soul is consistent reading and studying of Scripture. If you're a new Bible reader, be patient with yourself! Learn to study and apply God's Word one step at a time.

1. **Have your own Bible.** *Your own Bible is the one that has your name in it, the one that you not only carry to church, but even remember to bring home with you. You need a Bible that you cherish and keep close at hand.*

2. **Begin with prayer.** *Every time you sit down to read your Bible, ask God to speak to you through Scripture. Let Him know you are ready and willing to hear His voice.*

3. **Plan a Bible-reading schedule.** *You will profit more from Bible reading if you study entire books at a time, not just parts here and there. So map out a good Bible-reading schedule, planning which books to work through several at a time.*

4. **Use a study method.** *Discipline in Bible study is just like discipline in any other area—discipline leads to positive and healthy experiences in our lives.*

If you keep a notebook or prayer journal, you might start a section titled "My Time in the Word." As you learn one simple Bible study method, you'll see how a notebook can be used to make your time in the Word more effective.

Step One:

LOOK FOR THE BIG PICTURE

Before focusing on several verses of a particular chapter, get an overall idea of the book you are reading. Try to find out who is writing the book, to whom, and why. Many Bibles contain a short introduction to each book of the Bible with a lot of this information given. Another way to do this is to read the entire book quickly; if it is a longer book, simply skim through it and note the paragraph headings printed in your Bible. You're not trying to read every word, just get acquainted with the flow and feeling of the book.

Step Two:

SELECT A STUDY PASSAGE

Once you have an idea of the big picture, you'll want to study the entire book in chunks—anywhere from a few verses to an entire chapter at a time.

When you study a passage, what counts is quality of reading, not quantity. One caution: You will not want to break up paragraphs, or you will lose the writer's train of thought.

Step Three:

READ THE STUDY PASSAGE SEVERAL TIMES

After you choose the verses you are going to study, read that section of Scripture at least two times. Three or four times would be better. And remember, you set the pace—you can choose to study a chapter or just a few verses. What counts is that you grow in an understanding of God's Word.

Step Four:

SEARCH FOR MAJOR TRUTHS

As you read through your study passage for the third or fourth time, note the key thoughts found there. What does the writer want the people who read this to understand? Look for commands to be obeyed, warnings to be heeded, promises to be claimed, and truths to be believed.

Set aside a space in your journal for you to jot down these key thoughts and major truths.

Step Five:

ASK QUESTIONS

Now is the time to raise questions that come to your mind. Not everything in Scripture is immediately or easily understood. Do not be surprised or intimidated by this fact.

Write down your questions in your notebook or journal. Here are several places where you can go to get answers to these questions.

• **Scripture:** Use a concordance or study Bible to look up passages of Scripture that deal with the subject you're studying—often, one scripture can help explain another.

• **Commentaries:** Commentaries study and explain Bible passages a little at a time. Your church library probably contains several sets of commentaries you could borrow.

• **Pastors and teachers:** Your pastor and Sunday school teachers may not be able to give you an answer right away, but they will be willing to search for answers with you.

Step Six:

PUTTING IT INTO PRACTICE

You need to apply the Bible to your life now. "Do not merely listen to the word ... Do what it says" (1:22) was James' advice.

Is there something you are doing that you shouldn't be doing? Is there something you are not doing that you need to be doing? Is there something about God or Jesus or the Holy Spirit that you did not know before? Do you need to be more sensitive to someone at work? Do you need to seek someone's forgiveness? Do you need to forgive someone?

Step Seven:

NOTE A VERSE TO REMEMBER

The final step in your Bible study is to take one last look at your study passage and write down a verse or two that you want to remember most. Memorizing scripture is a terrific discipline. It allows you to take scripture with you, even when you don't or can't have your Bible at hand.

Writing out a key verse will make remembering it much easier for you. It is a good start to memorizing it also.

May God cause your soul to stretch and grow
as you embark on a journey through His Word!

Acknowledgements

"Confessions of a Martha" © Kathryn Lay. Used by permission. All rights reserved.

"God Knew" © Steffanie Clifton. Used by permission. All rights reserved.

"Treasures in Heaven" © Nanette Thorsen-Snipes. Used by permission. All rights reserved.

"Love Your Neighbor" © Karen R. Kilby. Used by permission. All rights reserved.

"A Sunshine Day" © Glenda Palmer. Used by permission. All rights reserved.

"Joy on a Hot June Day" © Edna Ellison. Used by permission. All rights reserved.

"What Does Joy Look Like?" © Carol Harrison. Used by permission. All rights reserved.

"Lord, Send Me a Friend" © Annettee Budzban. Used by permission. All rights reserved.

"Forgiveness or a Promissory Note?" © Judy Hampton. Used by permission. All rights reserved.

"From Mother-in-Law to Mother-in-Love" © Karen R. Kilby. Used by permission. All rights reserved.

"A Very Special Young Lady" © Nancy B. Gibbs. Used by permission. All rights reserved.

"A Little Honesty Goes a Long Way" © Kathryn Lay. Used by permission. All rights reserved.

"The Love of a Son" © Louise Tucker Jones. Used by permission. All rights reserved.

"When Perfectionism Causes Great Pains" © Kathy Collard Miller. Used by permission. All rights reserved.

"Follow Through" © Lynda Blair Vernalia. Used by permission. All rights reserved.

"Crutches One Day, Wings the Next" © Laurie Klein. Used by permission. All rights reserved.

"Which Weigh Did She Go?" © Candy Arrington. Used by permission. All rights reserved.

"My Son, the Prodigal" © Nanette Thorsen-Snipes. Used by permission. All rights reserved.

"From Mourning to Morning" © Louise Tucker Jones. Used by permission. All rights reserved.

"I'm Getting Older and Better" © Joan Clayton. Used by permission. All rights reserved.

Your Story

Has there been a time in your life when you encoun-
tered God in a powerful way that changed and
enriched your soul? Would your story encourage
others to grow closer to God and improve their lives?

WE WOULD LOVE TO CONSIDER YOUR STORY FOR FUTURE
EDITIONS OF SOUL MATTERS. PLEASE SHARE YOUR STORY
TODAY, WON'T YOU? FOR WRITER'S GUIDELINES, UPCOMING
TITLES, AND SUBMISSION PROCEDURES, VISIT:

www.soulmattersbooks.com

Or send a postage-paid, self-addressed envelope to:

**Mark Gilroy Communications, Inc.
6528 E. 101st Street, Suite 416
Tulsa, Oklahoma 74133-6754**